PATRICK HENRY, PATRIOT

WESTMINSTER PRESS BOOKS
BY TERI MARTINI

The Lucky Ghost Shirt
Patrick Henry, Patriot

PATRICK HENRY
PATRIOT

by Teri Martini

Illustrated by Robert Jacobson

THE WESTMINSTER PRESS
Philadelphia

PUBLISHED BY THE WESTMINSTER PRESS
®
PHILADELPHIA, PENNSYLVANIA

PRINTED IN THE UNITED STATES OF AMERICA

To Wendy with Love

Contents

1

A Big Decision

Patrick Henry arranged his fishing line between the toes of his bare right foot. He sighed with content and leaned back comfortably, resting his head against the trunk of a sturdy oak.

He did not hear the stealthy footsteps behind him. He did not see his brother William grinning to himself as he planned his surprise attack. For William Henry, it was now only a matter of watching and waiting.

Patrick was too absorbed by the sounds of spring to notice anything but the familiar songs of the birds — a cardinal, a robin, a catbird. He identified them easily.

Suddenly, Patrick felt a gentle tug on his line. The cork bobbed in the sparkling waters of Totopotomy Creek. With great care the boy raised himself to a sitting position. There was another tug on the line, harder, firmer.

A big one! Patrick stood to haul in his fish. As he did, there were wild shouts and cries that sounded as if the friendly Pamunkey Indian tribe had suddenly gone on the warpath. Patrick's line went slack. The fish was gone, frightened away.

Outraged, Patrick turned to face his older brother. William was so overcome with laughter that he rolled about on the ground. Instantly, twelve-year-old Patrick was upon him. The boys wrestled furiously. William was a year older and bigger. But Patrick had the blind strength that comes with anger. The two rolled about, punching and kicking until both of them were covered with dirt and grass.

All the while, Patrick's mind was working. He wasn't going to let William get away with such a low trick. He would have to teach Will a lesson. Patrick wrenched himself free.

"You're slow, Will," he taunted. "Too slow and lazy to catch me."

With that Patrick was off, racing barefoot through the woods. A quick glance behind him proved that Will had accepted the challenge.

Pleased with himself, the red-haired boy easily outdistanced his older brother. Patrick knew he could. All the boys said Patrick Henry was the fastest runner in Hanover County. Patrick himself thought he was probably the fastest runner in the entire colony of Virginia as well.

But now he deliberately slowed down so that William could catch up. Then when the older boy least expected it, Patrick stopped short. William tripped and went flying into a thicket of thorn bushes. Patrick meant to turn a somersault, jump to his feet, and taunt his brother. But he rolled over at an odd angle, and something cracked. For a moment the pain was so great that it made him too dizzy to stand.

William freed himself from the bushes and rushed over to continue the battle. One look at Patrick's face made him stop.

"What's wrong?"

"I . . . I don't know. Feels like something broke."

"Can you stand?" asked William anxiously.

"Maybe!"

Patrick tried, but the world seemed to grow dim around him. He sank to his knees.

"I'll carry you," said William.

With Patrick on his back, William slowly made his way up the side of the hill to Studley, their home. Patrick was much heavier than William had expected. Soon he knew he would never be able to get his brother to the house alone. When they had reached some of the outbuildings, William called to two Negro slaves.

"Patrick's hurt. Help me get him home."

Several hours later, the doctor came.

"It's a broken collarbone," he told Mrs. Henry.

"Will it mend?" asked the boy's mother. She was a lively woman with soft, dark hair that framed her lovely face.

"Oh, yes! But Patrick will have to stay home and rest quietly if he wants to have it mend properly."

Patrick groaned, but his mother ignored him. Sarah Henry had eight children. There was one boy, John Syme, Jr., from her first marriage. Then there were William, Patrick, and five little girls. She understood their moods.

"It will do Patrick good to rest quietly for a change," she said firmly. "He'll have time to catch up with the studying he has neglected."

Patrick groaned again. What a price to pay! And all because he wanted to teach William a lesson.

Patrick slept most of the day. But late in the afternoon his younger sister Jane came to the door with a tray.

"Are you hungry, Patrick?"

"Starved!" he answered, sitting up cautiously.

Jane placed the tray on his lap and arranged his pillows.

"That better?"

"I suppose so," Patrick answered in a dismal tone.

"Cheer up, Patrick. Things aren't so bad as they seem."

"No, they are worse. Nobody cares that I shall be cooped up in the house all the rest of the spring. I won't have a chance to go hunting or fishing. I hate everything."

Patrick turned his face to the pillow and sulked.

"Your biscuits are getting cold," said Jane.

"Who cares?"

"Then I'll just take them back," Jane reached for the tray.

"No, don't do that," said Patrick quickly. "I might be able to manage a few."

He looked slyly through long, dark lashes to see his sister's knowing smile. Soon they were both laughing.

Their high spirits did not last long. Colonel John Henry's boots were heard on the stairs.

"I think I had better go," said Jane.

Patrick knew she did not want to be around for the scolding he was bound to get.

Just before she left, Jane whispered, "Don't feel sad, Patrick. Mother is so sorry you are hurt that she is going to get you a flute."

A flute! That sounded promising. Patrick loved music. He played the fiddle rather well. Of course, he wouldn't be able to do that again until his bones healed. But perhaps he could manage a flute.

Colonel John Henry stood in the doorway and studied his second son as though he had never seen him before. Patrick squirmed under his steady gaze.

"What will become of you, Patrick?" said Colonel Henry at last. "You cannot spend your life roaming the woods like a wild Indian. You must learn to apply yourself to your studies. You must learn to be a gentleman."

Privately, Patrick thought he would rather be an Indian. It appeared to him that Indians had more fun.

Instead he said, "Yes, sir."

"Well, Patrick, we must make the most of our opportunities. During this enforced rest of yours I want you to think about what profession you will follow. There is nothing like striving for a goal to settle a man down." Papa drew a Latin grammar from his coat. "And now I think it is time for your lessons."

Ever since Patrick had left the English Common School when he was ten, his father had been his tutor. John Henry had been educated in Aberdeen, Scotland. He was a fine scholar and a good teacher. Patrick never did well at his studies. There were many more exciting things going on right in the woods than reading Latin and Greek and working with mathematics. Now it looked as though he would be doing more than his share of studying. Patrick sighed.

After the first day or two, the boy began to enjoy his rest. Mother had the cook make his favorite dishes. Papa gave him books to read, history mostly. Patrick found he enjoyed them. And then there were special visitors.

One visitor was Uncle Patrick, for whom the boy had been named. The Reverend Patrick Henry was the minister of St. Paul's Church.

"Well, young Patrick, how have you been occupying yourself?"

"Reading, Uncle Patrick, and thinking. Papa wants me to make an important decision."

"What is that?"

"He wants me to decide what I want to do with my life."

Rev. Henry shook his head slowly. "A serious decision indeed! What have you decided?"

"Nothing for certain, yet. But I have given thought to the ministry."

Rev. Henry was surprised and flattered that his nephew should want to follow his path in the service of God.

"What makes you think you would be suited to the ministry?"

"I like the preaching," said Patrick, his blue eyes sparkling. He launched into a marvelous imitation of all the ministers and all the sermons he had ever heard or read which appealed to him.

"How many of us cry, Peace, peace, to our souls, when there is no peace?"

Rev. Henry was amazed at Patrick's ability to repeat almost word for word parts of sermons he had heard weeks and months before. It was obvious that the boy liked the sound of words. He rolled them on his tongue as an orator would.

"I am impressed, Patrick, really impressed. But there is more to being a minister than preaching. There is the matter of doing God's work. In the end, it is God who chooses his ministers."

"Oh," said Patrick in a small voice.

As far as Patrick knew, the Lord had not called him. That did not mean He never would, of course. Patrick decided he would just have to wait and see.

Not long after Uncle Patrick's visit, Uncle William Winston came. Everybody called him "Langloo." The Indians with whom he often hunted had given him this name. Patrick admired Uncle Langloo more than anyone he knew. Uncle Langloo wore buckskin clothes and carried a long knife as well as a gun.

"Patrick! What's this? You are growing pale and weak, boy. You need exercise and fresh air," cried Uncle Langloo.

"I have to stay in until my bones mend," Patrick told him.

"Nonsense, boy, nonsense! Fresh air and exercise are what you need. Where is your mother? I'll tell her myself."

Patrick knew that it would be no use. His mother planned to keep him cooped up until the doctor pronounced him well. Patrick changed the subject.

"I've been thinking on what I'm going to be, Uncle Langloo. Papa wants me to decide. I think," his voice grew husky with excitement and his blue

eyes glowed, "I think I'd like to be like you, Uncle
Langloo. I want to be a hunter and a trapper. I
want to live with the Indians."

Uncle Langloo slapped his knee with pleasure.

"Why, boy, you couldn't choose a better life.
For adventure and excitement, you can't beat it.
But," he shook his head thoughtfully, "the frontier
is not the place for you. Not on a permanent basis."

"But . . . ," protested Patrick.

Uncle Langloo held up his hand.

"I know what you're going to say, Patrick. It's
true that you can track a deer as well as any young
Indian, and I have seen the traps you've made for
fish on your little creek here. But there's more to
frontier life than that. You live alone, far from your
family. Sometimes you don't see any other human
beings for weeks and months. No one to talk to,
Patrick, think of it! Do you realize how much you
like to talk? No, Patrick, that life is not for you."

No one to talk to for weeks and weeks! Patrick
had not thought about that. Maybe Uncle Langloo
was right.

By the time Patrick's collarbone healed, he had
read many books, caught up on his Latin and
Greek studies, and learned to play the flute. But
he still had no idea what he wanted to be.

2

Not Good for Business

As the first rays of the sun reached the small windows of the Henrys' General Store, Patrick closed his ledger and blew out the candle. He leaned back in the stiff, wooden chair, stretched and yawned. It was no use. No matter how he did the figuring, it always came out the same.

"We're in trouble, Will," he said, as his sleepy-eyed brother unlocked the door.

At eighteen William Henry was still bigger than Patrick. He was heavier, too. He loved to eat. Now he shook his head and blinked in surprise.

"What? You here already?"

"Couldn't sleep," said Patrick. "I'm worried, Will. Look at this."

He pointed to his neat columns of figures.

"We're in debt. Almost everyone owes us money."

William looked disgusted. "You gave up a good

night's sleep because of that? Everyone in Hanover County is in debt until harvest time. The farmers will pay us when they sell their crops."

"I know. I know," admitted Patrick. "But what if something goes wrong?"

"What if? What if?" mimicked William. "You are worrying about nothing, Patrick. Take off that long face. You'll frighten the customers away. Here! Have some cheese."

Patrick shrugged. Probably William was right. He accepted the food which his brother offered and ate it with relish. He had missed breakfast that morning.

Nearly two years earlier Colonel Henry concluded that young Patrick would never decide on a career himself. Patrick said he did not want to try farming. He did not think he had a calling to the ministry. And being a frontier trapper was not suitable as far as Colonel and Mrs. Henry were concerned.

At last John Henry apprenticed Patrick to a shopkeeper. After a year, William and Patrick became shopkeepers themselves. Colonel Henry invested his own money in a store for them. Now business did not appear to be very good.

Patrick was willing to forget all about business,

good or bad, when there was other talk at hand. That's what he liked most about shopkeeping. There was always plenty of opportunity to talk.

When the door opened and the first customer came in, Patrick set aside his troubles. The customer was George Dabney, a boy about his own age.

"Patrick Henry, you are the most energetic fellow I've seen in an age! How does he do it, Will?" asked the cheerful young man. "I believe he danced all night. He never sat down once. Not that I saw, anyway."

All three young men had been at a country dance given by John Syme, Jr., the boys' half brother. Patrick and William were living with John because his home was closer to the store than their own. The Henrys had moved a few years earlier to another plantation called Mount Brilliant.

"It's nothing for Patrick to dance all night," said Will. "He's a ladies' man."

"With eyes for only one lady, I think," said George slyly. "People are talking about you and Sarah Shelton, Patrick. She's a pretty lass."

Patrick felt his ears grow hot. They always did when he was embarrassed.

"Not so pretty as some," said Patrick. "Nor so plain as others."

He busied himself straightening shelves.

"Here, Will," he cried sharply. "What's this candle mold doing in with the snuff?"

He hoped the fellows would stop teasing. Patrick wasn't sure yet what he felt for Sarah. But the very mention of her name sent him into confusion.

Fortunately for Patrick, two more men came in. They were trappers.

"Trouble's coming, sure as Sunday," announced one, stamping his heavy boots.

"French trouble again?" asked Patrick, eager for news of the frontier.

"I should say! Why, those French will steal the animals right out of a man's trap," said the first fellow.

"I said it before, and I'll say it again. They have no right on the Ohio land. It's Virginia territory, and that land belongs to the King!" said the second man.

Patrick stretched out on a sack and settled himself for a good talk. Talk such as this bored William. He took a chair off to a corner, and in a few minutes he was fast asleep.

"The French are asking for trouble, and they are going to get it," said one of the trappers.

"You mean a fight?" asked Patrick.

Just then a man came into the store, looked about for a clerk, and spotted Patrick.

"I need some salt," said the man.

"Yes, sir," said Patrick, but he made no move to get it.

"Have you heard talk of war?" Patrick asked the trappers.

"There's talk of sending someone out to the French fort on the Ohio and ordering them to leave. They want to send a young fellow name of Washington."

"Salt," repeated the customer who had just come in. "I need some salt." He was becoming impatient.

"Certainly, sir," replied Patrick. But he went right on with his conversation. "The French would never leave without a fight, would they?"

"Won't somebody sell me some salt?" demanded the man.

"Salt?" said Patrick, annoyed at the interruption. "Salt? Sorry. I just sold the last peck."

He turned back to the trappers.

"Well, would the French give up the fort without a fight?"

The customer left, looking puzzled. A country store without salt was a strange place indeed.

"Say, Patrick," said George. "What is that you are sitting on? Isn't that a sack of salt?"

"Ha!" laughed Patrick. "So it is!"

The trappers roared with amusement. But everyone agreed that Patrick's carelessness was not good for business.

After the trappers and George had left, Patrick swept the floor. He opened the door and let the warm, fresh air blow through.

The little store was situated on a well-traveled road. But off to the west were the hills, beyond which was the wilderness. There were deer in the forest, partridges and wild duck along the river. The hills glowed with a golden, summer haze. Patrick could almost feel the silence of the woods and smell the scent of pine. In another minute he could stand it no longer. He threw down his broom.

"Will! Will!" he called excitedly.

The older boy woke with a start.

"What's wrong?"

"Nothing's wrong. Everything's right for hunting. Let's close up the store and go."

William did not have to be asked twice.

When customers came to the door later, they found it locked. It wasn't the first time the Henry boys had gone off hunting or fishing instead of

working. The people just shook their heads and
smiled.

But when Colonel John Henry arrived on a
surprise visit, he was not amused. He waited im-
patiently until the boys returned, and then he insisted upon seeing the account books.

"I was working on them this very morning,"
Patrick told his father virtuously, hoping that
would help to make up for the time they had spent
hunting.

"Before sunup, too," added Will helpfully.

"Hmm!" grunted Colonel Henry. He was not
impressed. He read the same sad story which Patrick had found in his figures.

"It appears to me you boys are in trouble. You
are way behind in your accounts."

"The farmers will pay come harvest time," said
Will as he had that morning.

"You can't wait until harvest time," Colonel
Henry told him angrily. "You will have to start col-
lecting something right away. This is no time for
frolicking in the woods. You get my meaning,
Patrick?"

Colonel Henry always looked to his younger
son for leadership. It was no secret that he thought
Patrick was more capable than William.

Patrick lowered his eyes. "Yes, sir," he said unhappily.

If there was one thing Patrick hated, it was having to collect money. But he determined to try. He did not want his father to be disappointed in him.

The first customer next morning was Mrs. Carter. Her husband ran a small tobacco farm, and they had five children. Patrick took a quick look at his ledger. The Carters owed twelve pounds.

"Morning, ma'am," said Patrick, smiling a welcome. "I haven't seen you in a long time."

"I have not been well, Patrick," said the lady. "My two youngest were down with croup. Mr. Carter had an accident. Cut his leg something awful. Could you let me have some supplies on credit?"

Patrick gulped. His ears grew hot.

"Well, ma'am, I would like to, but there already is a bill. You see, the fact is . . ."

Patrick's voice trailed off as he gazed into the woman's sad eyes.

"What supplies did you have in mind?" he asked.

Soon the counter was covered with the packages which made up Mrs. Carter's order. She smiled gratefully as she left.

"Don't worry, Patrick. We mean to settle our bill."

"Pay me when you can," said Patrick cheerfully. "Don't worry about the bill."

No matter how hard he tried, Patrick could not ask for money. The store had been open a little over a year. Harvest time had come and gone when Patrick and his father had another talk.

"Well, it's happened!" said Colonel Henry. "So many people owe you money that you can't pay your debts."

"That's what happens to storekeepers when crops are poor," pointed out Patrick. "The farmers don't have the money to pay."

Colonel Henry glowered at his son. "That's what happens when storekeepers don't tend to business," he said. "You'll have to sell your store. What now? I cannot afford to buy you another store."

Patrick was sorry that he had failed at storekeeping. He was sorry that his father had lost money. But he was young and hopeful. Surely something would turn up. He did not intend to be a failure all his life.

Patrick often talked his troubles over with Sarah Shelton. One evening he called for her in a

borrowed gig at the Shelton Farm, called Rural Plains. He was a steady visitor there. So were a number of other young men in the area. Still, Patrick was pleased to think that Sarah enjoyed his company more than she did most of the young men.

That evening Patrick laughed and joked, but it was not long before Sarah put her hand on his arm.

"What's wrong, Patrick?" she asked.

Patrick told her everything.

"I'm worried, Sarah," he said, looking into her sympathetic, dark eyes. "If I'm not good for shopkeeping, what can I do?"

Sarah looked up at him thoughtfully.

"You can do anything, Patrick. Anything at all. I believe in you."

Patrick was delighted. With a girl like Sarah at his side, he knew he could do anything.

Not long afterward Sarah Shelton and Patrick were married. He was only eighteen years old. She was two years younger. Ahead of them lay a lifetime.

Patrick determined to be successful at something. He wanted his family to be proud of him. Most of all he did not want to disappoint Sarah.

3

Law's the Thing

Patrick lifted his head and squinted at the position of the spring sun in the bright blue sky. He sighed and leaned on his hoe, wiping his forehead. There was still an hour until noon. Like the Negro slaves who worked beside him in the fields, Patrick looked forward to the big midday meal and a rest period. Farming was hard work.

"I don't mind the work," Patrick told his father-in-law. "But I wish I had something more to show for it, sir. My tobacco crops are poor. No doubt about it."

John Shelton had given Patrick and Sarah an important wedding gift. He gave them a 300-acre farm called Pine Slash, which adjoined his own lands. He added six Negro slaves as well. At eighteen, Patrick Henry had no means of supporting a family. Mr. Shelton had wanted to see the young couple off to a good start.

Although Patrick had always thought he would not like farming, he worked hard. Mr. Shelton was pleased with the way his young son-in-law endeavored to provide for his wife and child. Sarah and Patrick had a little girl, Martha, whom everyone called Patsy.

"You are doing well enough, my boy," Mr. Shelton told him. "You are new at farming. Don't be impatient. Give it time," he advised.

Patrick was willing to "give it time," but he felt discouraged. Now, resting on his hoe, he dreamed of the success he wanted to make of his life. There were so many things that he wanted to give Sarah and Patsy. A fine home was one thing, and the pretty clothes his wife loved so well was another.

"Master Patrick! Master Patrick!"

One of the slaves was racing toward him across the fields and shouting excitedly.

"Fire, Master Patrick!" cried the Negro.

Patrick looked up to see a column of smoke darken the sky above his wooden house. For a moment he froze.

Sarah and Patsy! A fire could sweep through a house like theirs quickly. Those inside could be trapped and burned to death.

Patrick threw down his hoe and fairly flew across the fields. He was relieved to find Sarah safely outside and holding Patsy in her arms.

Patrick organized the fight to save his home. He and his men worked for hours. Neighbors joined them. In the end the fire won, and Pine Slash burned to the ground.

That night the little family moved into the overseer's cabin.

"Farming isn't enough," Patrick told Sarah. "It will cost a good deal of money to rebuild the house. I'm going to try something else."

Sarah turned confident eyes to her husband. "Will we give up farming?"

She was certain that anything Patrick decided would be right.

Patrick rubbed the back of his head thoughtfully. "Not entirely," he said.

Then he jumped to his feet and began to pace the room excitedly.

"Look here, Sarah! I could sell some of our slaves and part of our land. I could set up a store in town. Maybe I could hire a clerk part-time. Then we would have an income from the farm and a store as well. How does that sound?"

"Wonderful!" cried Sarah with enthusiasm.

Patrick smiled. "What would I do without you, Sarah?"

"Papa! Papa!" cried a small voice. "Tell me a story."

"Patsy! What are you doing still awake?"

"It's a strange house and a strange bed," explained Sarah to her husband, as she smoothed the little girl's long curls.

Patsy was nearly three years old. Her hair and eyes were dark like her mother's. She also had Sarah's charm. Anything she asked of Patrick, he gave.

Now he swung the little girl up high toward the low, wooden ceiling of their makeshift home. Patsy squealed with delight.

"Not too much excitement," warned Sarah.

Patrick settled in a chair by the fire and told stories until little Patsy was fast asleep.

When Colonel Henry learned that Patrick was opening another store, he was surprised.

"Well, all I can say is, I hope you have learned something from your first experience."

Patrick certainly had, but times were bad. The Colonies were caught up in the war between England and France, called the French and Indian

War. The trappers had been right. The French would not leave the Ohio lands without a battle. Many of Virginia's men had volunteered to help fight for their rights on the frontier. If Patrick did not have so many family responsibilities, he, too, would have liked to join the fighting.

Like his father and other family men, Patrick was proud to serve in the militia. Once a week he took his gun and met with the small civilian army for drill. These men were well equipped to protect their homes. Sometimes, though, Patrick longed for the excitement of a real fight, especially after talking to Uncle Langloo, who had joined the army.

"You leave the fighting to us, boy," said Uncle Langloo. "We've had experience. We'll take care of the French. We'll clear them out of the Ohio land, and we'll make the frontier safe for honest trappers again."

Uncle Langloo paced about the small room like a caged bear.

"Why, those sneaking French have turned the Indians against us. Indians who once were my friends would now shoot me on sight. I tell you, I'm going to settle accounts."

British and colonial troops fought hard, but it

was a long war. And it cost money! Taxes were higher. People did not have much money to spend. Storekeepers did not make so many sales.

Then, too, French ships interfered with trade. Patrick was not able to get all the goods he needed for his store. He struggled along for two more years. Soon it was clear that he was poorer than ever. Now he and Sarah had two children. He would have to find some other way to make a living.

During the long winter months there was little work to be done on the farm. Patrick spent his time at the store. When there was no one about to discuss news of the war, Patrick spent his time reading and thinking. He had not made a success of himself yet. But he was still hopeful.

In December, Sarah and Patrick received an invitation from Colonel Nathaniel West Dandridge to spend the Christmas holidays at his home.

"Let's go, Patrick," said Sarah. "Bring home some taffeta and ribbons from the store. I'll make a new dress. We'll forget our troubles."

House parties at the homes of wealthy planters, such as Colonel Dandridge, were gay affairs. They often lasted several weeks. There would be interesting people, good talk, and fun.

"I'll bring my fiddle," said Patrick happily.

As always, Patrick was a favorite at the party. He told stories, danced with the ladies, and played his fiddle. Colonel Dandridge had a little daughter Patsy's age. Her name was Dorothea, Dolly for short. She liked Patrick's stories every bit as much as Patsy did.

Patrick noticed one guest in particular. He was a tall young man who looked to be about seventeen. His hair was as red as Patrick's, and he seemed amiable, but shy. His name was Thomas Jefferson.

Patrick liked to see people enjoy themselves.

"Here, Jefferson," he said one evening, swinging his fiddle under his arm. "Didn't I see a violin case about you when you arrived? Where is it now?"

"Why . . . why, in my room," replied the startled young man.

"Well, go and get it, Jefferson. Fiddling is hard work, and there are a large number of people here just waiting to dance. You can't expect me to handle the job of making music all alone."

Thomas Jefferson laughed. Colonel Dandridge hardly needed either of them to entertain the guests. He had hired musicians. But Thomas loved

music. He got his violin and his music case as well.

As Thomas spread the music on a stand, Patrick frowned and pointed to it with his bow.

"What's this, Jefferson?" he asked.

"My music. I've copied some of the popular songs of the day. You are welcome to use it, if you like, Mr. Henry."

Patrick laughed, and his blue eyes twinkled.

"Well, thanks all the same, Jefferson, but I don't read music. I play by ear. That's my method. Why don't you start in, and when I catch the melody, I'll join you."

Patrick and Thomas got on well together. Although Patrick was seven years older than Thomas, they found they could talk together for hours. They speculated on how long it would take before the frontier lands were really cleared of French trappers. They wondered, too, how the colonists were going to pay for the war. England would expect them to share the expense.

Patrick spoke very little of himself. When Thomas asked about the older man's interests, Patrick merely shrugged.

"Oh, a little of this and a little of that. I've tried farming, and I've tried shopkeeping. Neither was much of a success. But something will turn up soon," he added cheerfully. "What about you, Jefferson? What are your plans?"

"I'm going to Williamsburg," Thomas told him. "I plan to study at the College of William and Mary."

"Ah! I hear that our capital is a lively city. Not the sort of place to study. There are dances, races, and the theater. When the Burgesses are there for spring and fall sessions, you'll want to see our colonial government in action. No, you won't get much studying done."

"Perhaps," said Thomas. "But I'll do my best to concentrate on my books. I may stay on after my first two years. I may study law."

Patrick nodded appreciatively. "How long will that take?"

"Oh, three or four years."

Patrick shook his head. "Three or four years!" he exclaimed. "That's an uncommonly long time. I wouldn't have the patience for that. If I made up my mind to study law, I would get all the books I needed and study for six or seven weeks straight."

"You're joking, Mr. Henry!" Thomas searched his friend's face to see if this were true.

"Not at all, Mr. Jefferson. That's the way I would do it. What interests you about the law?"

As Thomas spoke enthusiastically, Patrick began to think seriously about this profession. He loved to argue, and he was good at it. He wondered whether this quality might not make him a good lawyer.

"Sarah," he said, that evening when they retired to their room. "What kind of lawyer do you think I would make?"

Sarah smiled fondly at her husband. "The best in Virginia," she told him, and she meant it.

"You know, Sarah, you may be right."

When the holidays were over, Patrick began to think about getting rid of his store. It certainly was not making money. He and his family were now living in rooms at Shelton's Tavern in Hanover. Patrick helped his father-in-law to serve in the tavern, and at the same time, he enjoyed long talks with the customers.

But now, late at night and early in the morning, Sarah would find Patrick poring over lawbooks which he had borrowed. He found he enjoyed the challenge of this study more than anything he had done so far. Patrick began to feel that at last he had found work that he could thoroughly enjoy. Perhaps he was going to be a success after all.

4

A Difficult Test

March came to Hanover. Local farmers and merchants traveled to town for the opening of court. Although the court met the first Thursday of every month, there were only four large sessions during the year in March, June, September, and December.

Patrick was anxious for this session to begin. He wanted to test his knowledge against that of experienced lawyers. For days the courthouse would be the busiest place in town. Patrick planned to hear as many cases as he could.

"Now that I have studied the Lawyers' Bible," he told his friend, John Lewis, "I want to see the law in action again."

John Lewis was a country lawyer and an old friend. He was one of the few people who knew that Patrick was reading law. In those days there were no law schools. A man who wanted to become a lawyer studied with an established member of the bar. Patrick had borrowed the necessary books and had done the studying on his own.

"The Lawyers' Bible!" John Lewis chuckled, as he thought of the text, *Coke on Littleton.*

"That is one of the dullest books in the English language. Yet none is of more value to a lawyer. If you have mastered that on your own, you are ready to try for your license."

Every time Patrick thought of being examined by highly respected Williamsburg lawyers, his knees felt weak. But he would have to face them if he wanted his license. Patrick went to the courthouse each day. He had to thread his way among traveling acrobats, peddlers, and hawkers. Children were everywhere. Women stood about gossiping and shopping.

"See the fighting contest tonight!" shouted a man.

Patrick grinned. He planned to go. Afterward, Shelton's Tavern would be crowded with men reliving the fight. The people of Hanover enjoyed a little recreation along with their legal business.

Once inside the courthouse Patrick listened to

lawyers plead for money owed to their clients. He heard long, sometimes amusing testimony concerning slander.

"Why, that fellow called me a chicken stealer! It's like to ruin my reputation," complained one farmer before the court.

His lawyer won the case, and the man was awarded twenty pounds for the damage to his character.

For each case Patrick formulated a plan for handling the lawsuit. Then he watched the lawyers critically. Sometimes they seemed to follow the same tactics. Sometimes they did not. But even when they did not, Patrick was satisfied that he could have won the case his way.

At last he went back to John Lewis.

"I'm ready," he announced. "Whom do I see about getting the license?"

"Robert Carter Nicholas, probably. Then there are the Randolphs, John and Peyton. You can try George Wythe, as well. They are all prominent lawyers. You will need two signatures for your license."

John Lewis rose and put a friendly arm around Patrick's shoulders.

"You have a sharp mind, Patrick. I am convinced that you have ability. Don't let those fancy Williamsburg lawyers throw a scare into you."

Patrick managed a weak smile.

"I'll try," he said.

At home he showed only confidence. There was no need to worry Sarah.

"Oh, Patrick, I wish you would wait until the spring rains are over," Sarah said. "It will be a muddy, uncomfortable ride to Williamsburg. You are liable to take a chill."

Patrick laughed. "Sarah! Have you ever known me to take a chill? Besides, the sooner I go, the sooner I can begin practicing law."

Tucking a few lawbooks into his saddlebags for last-minute study, Patrick left Hanover. He arrived in Williamsburg a few days later. There he found an inexpensive room and did what he could to remove the mud from his clothes. Then he set off to see the city. He headed immediately for Duke of Gloucester Street. It was the main street, a wide, tree-lined avenue. At one end was the magnificent House of Burgesses, where Virginia government was carried on. At the other end was the College of William and Mary. There Patrick found

his young friend Thomas Jefferson.

Thomas was very much surprised to see Patrick.

"You must let me show you the city," he said. "But what brings you to Williamsburg?"

"The law," announced Patrick, settling himself in a comfortable chair. "I've come to get my license."

Thomas could hardly believe his ears. Patrick Henry had not been joking that evening at Colonel Dandridge's home. He had made an amazingly rapid study of the required texts.

"Are you sure you are ready?" Thomas asked doubtfully.

"As ready as I shall ever be. Could you show me the way to the home of George Wythe? I'll want to make an appointment to see him."

Thomas took his friend there immediately. Later, on their tour of the city, he showed Patrick the fine homes of the other lawyers as well.

Patrick was greatly impressed by the magnificent governor's palace.

"I understand that it was designed by Governor Spotswood. That would be Mrs. Dandridge's father, wouldn't it?" asked Thomas.

"Yes, it would," replied Patrick. "I'd like to see

the office of the *Virginia Gazette*. You know, Sarah's grandfather founded the newspaper and started the bookstore. He was a family success that I have to live up to."

Thomas was amused. Patrick Henry looked like anything but a success. His clothes were shabby and rumpled from his long journey. They were far from fashionable, and he wore no powdered wig.

Besides that, Patrick talked with a slow, country drawl that would not be considered cultured by Williamsburg standards. Still, he seemed so sure of himself that Thomas could not help believing in the older man.

Of the four lawyers Patrick saw, only two signed his license. One of these men was John Randolph.

John Randolph was an elegant man who was always dressed in the height of fashion. He was only nine years older than Patrick, but he was one of the wealthiest men in the colony. Mr. Randolph took one look at Patrick Henry and dismissed him in his mind as an ignorant backwoodsman.

"I don't think a legal examination would be worth the trouble for either you or me," he said haughtily.

Patrick did not appear to be discouraged. He smiled, and with great charm convinced the lawyer to grant him a hearing.

"Mr. Randolph, there isn't a man in all Virginia who does not admire you. I have long wanted to meet you, hardly daring to hope that such a meeting would ever take place. My license has already been signed, but imagine the prestige that would be added with your signature."

Mr. Randolph was flattered. He was surprised to learn that anyone had signed Patrick's license. He began to wonder if he had misjudged the young man. The interview was granted.

To hear Patrick's smooth, confident tone, no one would have suspected that he was fighting a severe attack of nervousness. He had already learned from other lawyers he had visited that his preparation was very poor. The only reason he obtained the first signature on his license was that he had promised fervently to prepare himself further.

Now Mr. Randolph quickly found that Patrick's knowledge of common law was not adequate.

"History seems to be your strong area, Mr. Henry," he said.

"That's something, anyway, thought Patrick.

At least Mr. Randolph did not find him completely uneducated. By now, though, Patrick had little hope of getting the second signature needed for his license.

Then Mr. Randolph launched into a discussion of fine legal points. Patrick had little upon which to base his arguments but common sense. This he did with enthusiasm and originality. Mr. Randolph was impressed.

"We have been arguing a principle of law which I cannot clearly recall," said Mr. Randolph. "Come into my office, Mr. Henry. Let us look it up in the lawbooks. We shall see which of us is correct in his argument."

Mr. Randolph was astonished to find that Patrick with his scant knowledge had been right all the time.

"I shall sign your license, Mr. Henry. You are a man of natural genius. What knowledge you do not have, I am certain you will acquire."

Patrick breathed a heavy sigh of relief. He was a licensed lawyer at last.

"You may be interested to know that I have learned a valuable lesson myself today," said Mr.

Randolph, as Patrick was preparing to leave.

"What is that?"

"If you will forgive me for saying so, I have learned not to judge by appearances."

For the first time Patrick realized the impression which his worn and rumpled clothes must have made.

"Rest assured, Mr. Randolph, that I shall endeavor to correct that fault as well," he promised solemnly.

But it was a long time before Patrick could afford to honor that pledge. He returned to Hanover in triumph. Sarah, Patsy, and young John watched proudly as he hung his name on the Shelton Tavern door.

Then they waited. When no one came to him with a case the first day, Patrick was disappointed.

"People are not ready to think of you as a lawyer yet, my boy," his father in-law told him. "The men are used to thinking of you as a farmer and the proprietor of a store. They see you helping me serve in the tavern. It is hard for them to get used to the idea."

Patrick did not have to wait too long. On April 10, he entered a plea for a client at Goochland

Courthouse. Mr. Webber was suing Mr. Harding for thirty pounds. Patrick entered the plea for Mr. Webber and won. It was his first victory.

For three years Patrick handled many such small cases. They did not pay well, but he felt that he was gaining valuable experience. He used his free time to study. Still, he wished he could do more for his family.

"I want to give you a home of your own again," he told Sarah.

"I have all I want," Sarah answered. "You and the children make me happy."

But Patrick was not satisfied. What he needed to be a success was an important case! He needed the kind of case that people would talk about.

5

A Success at Last

On a fine autumn day in 1763 Patrick drove his
family to Mount Brilliant, his father's home, for a
visit. The green Virginia hills had turned scarlet
and gold. They seemed to glow against the azure
blue of the sky.

The horses pulling the small open carriage
pranced along gaily, as Patrick Henry, suddenly
filled with high spirits, threw back his head and
began to sing.

Startled, Sarah looked about her anxiously and
tugged at her husband's sleeve. Patrick broke off
in the middle of a line.

"What's wrong?" he asked innocently.

"What if we met one of your clients along the
road?" asked Sarah. "It's . . . it's not dignified for a
lawyer to ride about the hills singing. What will
people think?" She adjusted her bonnet self-con-
sciously.

Patrick's blue eyes twinkled.

"Think? What will people think?" he asked. "Why, they'll think, there goes Patrick Henry. He's in fine spirits, a regular fellow. Nothing stuffy about him."

Young John clapped his hands.

"Sing 'The Frog and the Mouse,' Papa."

Patrick complied good-naturedly, watching Sarah's disapproving expression from the corner of his eye. Soon Sarah's expression changed to amusement. By the time they had reached Mount Brilliant, they were all singing. Patsy and Sarah added their sopranos. John hummed a good deal because he kept forgetting the words. And the baby, William, merely added to the racket with whatever sound was easiest.

"You know, Sarah," said Patrick, "I used to dread these visits."

Sarah was surprised. "You always seemed to enjoy yourself."

Patrick shrugged. "Where there is good food, good music, and good talk a man can always enjoy himself. No, I was not comfortable. I always felt that my father was disappointed in me. But now," Patrick paused and grinned. "Well, now things are different."

Sarah touched her husband's arm affection-
ately. She did not have to say anything.

Colonel Henry had reason to be proud of both
his sons these days. William was married and had
settled down at last. And Patrick had taken his
law business seriously.

"You never cease to amaze me," Colonel Henry
told his son as they went for a stroll about the
grounds later. "I thought you would never amount
to anything. And now look at you!"

"Oh, don't do that," said Patrick. "Appearances
are so deceiving."

Colonel Henry laughed, and they sat down on
a wooden bench to rest. Relaxed and unguarded
now, John Henry's expression betrayed the con-
cern that he had been trying to hide.

Patrick suspected that his father was disturbed
about something. Perhaps the older man was not
well.

"What is it, Father?" he asked.

"I'm in debt, Patrick. Times are bad for
farmers. My tobacco crop was poor this season, and
taxes are high. They've eaten into my small profit.
I've been doing some tutoring here and there. It is
not enough."

"Is that all?" Patrick was so relieved to find that

his father was not ill that he could not help treating the matter lightly.

Colonel Henry frowned disapprovingly at his son. "All! Why, I'll have to sell some of my land to satisfy my creditors! This is no time for jokes."

"But I can help you easily," Patrick said, pleased to be able to make the offer. "I've been able to save some money. You are welcome to it."

Patrick's father was reluctant to accept his son's money, but the young man's powers of persuasion were great.

"I'll never have a better opportunity to repay you for the investment you made in our store."

At last Colonel Henry gave in. There was little else he could do.

A few days later Patrick had a visit from his brother in-law, Samuel Meredith. Colonel Meredith was married to Patrick's sister Jane and owned land not far from Mount Brilliant.

"To tell you the truth, Patrick, I am worried. Now that the Twopenny Act was declared not a law by Hanover court, small merchants and farmers are going to be in worse trouble than ever. Can't something be done?"

In November of 1763 everyone in Hanover was

talking about the Twopenny Act. This law was passed by the people of Virginia to enable them to pay their ministers in money instead of tobacco.

The ministers of the Church of England had to be supported by the colony. Many of the people did not even attend this church. But the King's law said that the ministers must be paid in tobacco. Everyone must share the expense.

Because tobacco was so valuable, the crop was often used instead of money. When harvests were poor, farmers found it a hardship to pay their ministers in tobacco. The people influenced the Assembly to pass the Twopenny Act. The ministers immediately complained to the King.

"The Colony of Virginia has no right to change a royal order," was King George's answer.

With the support of their King, several angry ministers were suing the people for money. The clergy insisted upon receiving their back pay. In Hanover County the Reverend James Maury brought his case to court. It was known as the Parson's Cause.

"I have been following the case, Sam," said Patrick. "There is very little that can be done now. It is up to the jury to decide how much the people owe Rev. Maury. Then taxes will be collected to make up the amount."

Sam passed a weary hand over his eyes. "More money!" he said. "Where will we find this money?"

Patrick did not see how he could help. But that evening he had a visit from Tarleton Brown and George Johnston. These men were the collectors for Rev. Maury's parish. Rev. Maury was suing them for his back pay. They both looked grim and determined when they arrived.

"We've come on business," George Johnston told Patrick briskly.

"John Lewis has resigned from our case," Tarleton Brown said. "He feels it is hopeless. We know this is short notice, Mr. Henry, but do you think you can help us?"

Patrick was almost too surprised to say anything. The chances of Rev. Maury being awarded a very large amount of money must be excellent, or else John would not have withdrawn.

"I haven't had much experience," Patrick told the men frankly. "I don't know whether I am ready to handle something as difficult as this."

"You've handled some work for me," said Mr. Johnston, "and I have been satisfied. Maybe a young, original mind is just what we need."

Still Patrick hesitated. There was so much interest in this case that he might be open to a great deal of criticism. Because he did not believe the Twopenny Act was wrong, he might have to speak out against the King. This was a dangerous thing to do. In the past, people were put in jail or hanged for such a crime.

Patrick remembered his talk with Sam. He thought of his own father's difficulties. Where would the small farmers and merchants get more money?

"All right," said Patrick. "Gentlemen, I will do my best."

There was little time to prepare the case, but Patrick worked hard. By December 1, 1763, he was satisfied that everything was ready, but he was not at all certain of the outcome.

Sam Meredith, who was staying at Shelton's Tavern so that he could be present in court, walked across the square that morning with Patrick.

"Have you ever seen so many ministers all in one place before?" asked Sam as they observed the dark-robed members of the clergy entering the courthouse.

"Never," said Patrick.

He found he had to fight to keep his voice
steady. Patrick thought he had never been so ner-
vous before in his life. No other case in years had
drawn such a large number of people. Then, too,
Colonel John Henry would be one of the presiding
justices. Patrick wanted especially to do well for
his father's sake. He did not want to embarrass
Colonel Henry before his friends and neighbors.

"Look, Patrick," cried Sam suddenly. "Isn't
that your uncle?"

Patrick looked up to see Rev. Henry driving
toward the courthouse in his carriage.

"Oh, no!" cried Patrick. This was too much. He
hurried to his uncle's side.

"I must beg a favor of you, Uncle," he said.

Rev. Patrick Henry beamed down at his
nephew. "What is that, young Patrick?"

"Please go home."

Rev. Henry raised his brows. "Go home! But
I've come a long way to be present. Many of my
colleagues are here. And I am anxious to hear you
speak before a jury. You would not deny me that
pleasure." The older man smiled confidently.

"But we are on opposite sides!" argued Patrick.
"I may have to say some harsh things about the
ministry. Please, Uncle! It would upset me to have

you present. Please don't go in."

The minister gazed thoughtfully at his nephew's worried expression. It was obvious that Patrick was terribly concerned.

"Very well, I don't want to upset you." He turned the carriage around and drove off.

Patrick was greatly relieved. "I don't think I could have spoken a word with Uncle Patrick there," he told Sam.

The trial began when Rev. Maury's lawyer, Peter Lyons, rose and demanded the minister's back pay.

Patrick offered in evidence a receipt for the money Rev. Maury had already been paid. Then he sat down. The spectators gasped aloud. Is that all Patrick was prepared to do?

Peter Lyons rose again.

"I concede that Rev. Maury was paid a salary, but it was hardly adequate. If he had been paid in tobacco, he would have received three times this amount."

Mr. Lyons went on to speak about the Two-penny Act, and how wrong the people of Virginia were to pass this act over the ruling of their King.

Peter Lyons had made a serious mistake, although he did not realize it. When he sat down

again, he was sure that the case had been won for
his client. He did not expect Patrick to have an
argument, but he was wrong.

Patrick rose slowly to his feet. He looked
around the courtroom. He dared not meet his
father's eyes. He looked instead at the ministers
who filled the first several rows of benches. They
looked extremely forbidding. Slowly, hesitantly,
Patrick began to speak.

His voice was low, for he was unsure of himself. Who was he to oppose the ministers of the
King's Church? People strained and shifted noisily
in their seats, trying to hear him. Then Patrick
looked at the back of the courtroom. He saw
friends and neighbors there. These were the people
who would suffer if the jury awarded the parson
a large sum of money. They were depending on
Patrick Henry.

Suddenly the young lawyer stood tall and
thrust up his chin proudly.

"We are free Englishmen, with all the rights of
Englishmen. What does King George know about
the problems of small farmers in Virginia?" he
asked.

Everyone in the courtroom became very quiet.

Patrick Henry dared to challenge the King of England.

"I am happy that Mr. Lyons introduced the subject of the Twopenny Act," Patrick went on.

"Laws must be obeyed. I do not deny this. But the welfare of the people is the supreme law. When laws cause hardships, they must be changed. That is why I feel the Assembly had every right to pass the Twopenny Act."

Patrick's voice was firm and clear as he developed his point. He used examples with which they were familiar. When he asked questions, the people shook their heads in answer. When he was indignant, the men were indignant. When he was proud, they were proud. Never had anyone so captured a jury or an audience.

"Is it fitting for ministers of the church, which teaches men to help the poor and feed the hungry, to ask money from the poor farmer who has none to give?" demanded Patrick.

Delighted, the farmers, many of whom were already in debt, cheered. Outraged, the clergy marched from the courtroom together. Patrick was not disturbed.

"The Twopenny Act has been declared not a

law," Patrick told the jury. "I cannot argue that fact. You must, therefore, award Rev. Maury what you think he deserves. But, you need not award him any more than a farthing!"

Patrick concluded his speech and sat down.

Slowly, as if awakening from a dream, the jury left the room. They returned in a matter of moments. They had decided to award Rev. Maury one penny.

How the people cheered! They rushed forward and carried Patrick away on their shoulders.

That evening when he returned home, Patrick found Sarah waiting for him.

"Oh, Patrick, how wonderful!" she cried. "I knew that someday you would be a success, and now you are!"

"It looks like it, doesn't it?" said Patrick, smiling modestly. "Sarah, perhaps I ought to go into government. Do you think anyone would vote for me?"

6

A Bold Move

As a lawyer, Patrick Henry was suddenly in great demand. He had won an important case just as he had always hoped he would. People considered him a hero, and in Shelton's Tavern the story of his speech in the Parson's Cause was told over and over again.

Patrick enjoyed his popularity, but he continued to work hard. Now, when people heard that Mr. Henry would be at court, they flocked to hear him speak. He was greatly admired by men of Hanover and Louisa Counties.

Soon he found that he had earned enough money to buy a home of his own again.

"I've bought some land, Sarah," he announced one day. "You'll like it. It's over in Louisa County, out in the country. There's a fresh stream flowing through it. They call it Roundabout Creek."

Sarah set aside her sewing. She had waited for this day a long time.

"When can we move?"

"Late spring, I should think. The house will be ready by then."

"Can we fish in our own creek? "asked young John eagerly.

Patrick ruffled his son's reddish hair. "I should say we can. And we'll hunt in our own woods, too. Soon you will be old enough for a gun of your own."

Before the Henrys actually moved to Louisa County, Patrick received an unexpected offer. He was staying in Louisa County for a few days while working on cases he had taken there. One evening some men took him to dinner.

"Look here, Patrick, you're the kind of man we need. You won't be afraid to speak out for the small farmers in Williamsburg. We want you to stand for election to the House of Burgesses," they told him.

"Go into government? Would I get enough votes?" asked Patrick.

When he had suggested this to Sarah more than a year before, he had been joking. It was obvious, though, that these men were serious.

"Not get enough votes?" One man laughed and slapped Patrick on the back. "Why, I wouldn't be surprised if you were the most popular man in Hanover as well as in Louisa County. What do you say?"

There was only one thing Patrick could say.

"If the people want me, I'm willing to serve."

Late in May, Patrick Henry was in Williamsburg. He had been elected to the House of Burgesses to replace William Johnson, who had resigned. Patrick was nearly overwhelmed by this responsibility. The House of Burgesses was the oldest lawmaking body in the Colonies. The other Colonies looked to Virginia for leadership. What kind of contribution could he make to such an important assembly?

When Patrick arrived, the streets of the city were crowded, as they always were during the spring session. Carriages rumbled along the dusty roads. Patrick caught glimpses of ladies in bright-colored silks and satins. Gentlemen, wearing fine velvet suits with cuffs of delicate lace, strolled along the brick walks. In vain Patrick searched for a friendly face among them. But no one seemed to notice the slim young man in the plain, dark suit and dusty boots.

As soon as he could, Patrick went to see his friend Thomas Jefferson. Thomas was pleased to hear of Patrick's election.

"There are only nine days left in this session, though. I guess you won't be able to get much done in that time."

"Oh, I don't know," said Patrick. "It seems to me we will have something important to talk about. There's the Stamp Act. What are people saying about it here?"

News of the Stamp Act had just reached the colonies. It had been passed by the British Parliament in March 1765, over a great deal of protest from the colonial representatives in England. In December, Virginia had sent a series of resolutions protesting the law to Parliament.

Interest sparkled in Thomas Jefferson's eyes.

"The Stamp Act! Now there is a cause! It will take real initiative and imagination to tackle that. Everyone is grumbling about it, but no one has a plan of action so far as I can see. Come with me and hear for yourself what men are saying."

They went to a local tavern. There the talk

soon turned to colony politics.

"Stamps on birth certificates! Stamps on my newspapers! Stamps to get married," grumbled one man.

"Stamps to die!" said another. " A death certificate is paper, too, you know."

Everyone laughed, but to the colonists of Virginia the Stamp Act would be a real burden.

Following the close of the French and Indian War, England needed money. Since the war was fought to protect the rights of the colonists from the French on the frontier, the English thought that the colonists should help to pay for it. Instead of asking the colonists to do this, England chose to tax them. The tax was in the form of stamps to be put on all paper purchased in the Colonies. These stamps would be paid for with silver, and that was scarce. Rich as well as poor would feel this tax. No one liked the idea.

"It seems as though men feel the same way here as they do in Hanover," said Patrick. "And it seems as though someone should do something about this Stamp Act."

"What can be done?" asked Thomas. "It's already a law. I don't think any member of the House of Burgesses will dare touch the subject, would you?"

The next day Patrick went to his first session in the House of Burgesses. The chamber was paneled in oak. Speaker Robinson sat in a magnificent high-backed chair at the far end of the room beneath a round window. Facing each other on opposite sides of a long table were double rows of wooden benches. Here is where the representatives sat. They hardly noticed their newest member, as Patrick Henry quietly took his place among them.

Each day Patrick expected someone to bring up the Stamp Act for discussion. Which of the respected leaders would it be? George Wythe was a thoughtful man and a brilliant lawyer. Surely he would speak out against this injustice. Or perhaps Peyton Randolph, one of the wealthiest men in the colony, would voice a formal protest. Patrick was ready to support any leader with the courage to speak. But no one did.

In talking privately with two other members, John Fleming and George Johnston, Patrick found that they, too, were hoping that something would be said. Time was slipping by.

Patrick decided upon a bold move. He had

been elected to represent the people of Louisa County. He knew how they felt about the Stamp Act. It would be wrong for him to remain silent. Even though it was dangerous to speak out, he must do it.

"I have prepared something," Patrick told his friends. "I wonder what you would think of my idea."

On a blank paper he had torn from an old law-book, Patrick had hastily written some resolutions. There were seven of them.

1. As Englishmen, Virginia colonists brought to the New World all the rights and privileges of Englishmen.
2. Two royal charters confirm that the colonists are entitled to the rights of Englishmen.
3. Only the people themselves know what taxes they can pay and what method is best for raising them.
4. The people of Virginia always enjoyed the right to make their own laws.
5. The General Assembly of the colony has the right to lay taxes, and any attempt to take this right away destroys American freedom.

6. The colonists are not bound to pay any tax but what they themselves make.

7. Any persons who maintain that others have the right to tax the Colonies are enemies of this colony.

Mr. Johnston whistled softly. "Do you propose to read these before the Burgesses yourself?"

Patrick nodded. "No one else seems inclined to say anything."

"Many are afraid," said John Fleming. "Aren't you? Resolutions such as these will sound like treason. They defy Parliament and the King."

"I realize the danger," said Patrick. "If the King tries to have me arrested, I plan to seek safety in the back country. I am satisfied that the people of Hanover and Louisa Counties will help me. In any case, my cause is just. I see no reason to hesitate."

"I, for one," said George Johnston, lifting his head in defiance, "would be proud to have Virginia be the first colony to notify the Crown of our true feelings. If you have the courage to speak, Mr. Henry, I will support you."

"As will I," promised John Fleming. "And may heaven help us."

Thomas Jefferson, who had been visiting the House almost every day since Patrick had arrived, was certain that the members were going to ignore the Stamp Act.

"There are only three days left," he said to Patrick. "So many of the members have already left I wonder whether there will be a third of the men present tomorrow. No one seems to be expecting any excitement."

Patrick gave his young friend a mysterious look.

"Don't give up. The session isn't over yet."

And so Thomas Jefferson was present the next day when Patrick read his resolutions. It was the morning of May 29, 1765, Patrick's twenty-ninth birthday. The speech was so important to him that Patrick hardly noticed what day it was.

He stood before the Burgesses and made his bold move almost casually. To everyone's amazement the men voted to consider the resolutions. Then the battle began, and it went on for three days.

The older members were not in favor of such drastic statements. They were annoyed that a newcomer from the back country had taken the leadership from them.

"We are Englishmen and must obey English law," said George Wythe.

"As Englishmen, with the rights of Englishmen, we must protest this act of Parliament. We were not consulted in the matter of this tax. It is being forced upon us," cried Patrick.

Peyton Randolph rose slowly to his feet. "Above all," he said carefully, " we are gentlemen. These," he gestured with distaste toward Patrick's paper, "resolutions are the rash act of a young and inexperienced, country lawyer."

Mr. Randolph emphasized the word "country" expressively. Patrick felt the insult, but he could not let it bother him now. Evidently the Randolphs often made the mistake of judging by appearances. Patrick had proved John Randolph wrong. He could do the same for Peyton.

"The King," continued Mr. Randolph, "will come around to our way of thinking in time."

In time! Patrick wondered how long Mr. Randolph expected the Colonies to wait. A year? Two years? In the meantime they were living under the rule of a tyrant. Tyrants, history had shown, risked assassination by their suffering, indignant people.

Patrick leaped to his feet. His eyes burned with anger. His full, rich voice filled the room.

"Caesar had his Brutus; Charles the First, his Cromwell," he cried.

Several members shouted furiously, "Treason! Treason!"

Standing in the doorway, Thomas Jefferson caught his breath. Would Patrick Henry dare to suggest that King George should be put to death as Caesar and King Charles the First had?

Patrick stood firm in the face of these accusations. He held his head high and continued in a loud voice.

"And George the Third may profit by their example. If this be treason," he added, "make the most of it."

Richard Henry Lee, George Johnston, and John Fleming jumped to Patrick's assistance. They argued for the resolutions valiantly. In the end, five of them were passed and sent to the King. The sixth and seventh were considered too strong.

Late in the afternoon of May 30, the younger members of the House of Burgesses celebrated their victory. Patrick changed into his rough, buckskin breeches, packed his clothes, and started quietly for home.

His resolutions were printed and sent to all the Colonies. Soon many people heard of his stirring speech. Before, people had only grumbled among themselves about the Stamp Act. Now they real-

ized that something could be done about it. Patrick
had made the first bold move that gave men courage. Not long afterward, Parliament repealed the
Stamp Act.

Patrick's action was not without danger. His
name was soon known to the King and to Parliament. To them he was a criminal. Had he been in
England, they might have hanged him. From now
on, Patrick Henry would be watched carefully.

7

Outsmarting the King

Sarah Henry paced the rooms of her new home and gazed at the unfinished walls in dismay. When Patrick joked about Roundabout being like the edge of the wilderness after Hanover, he had not been far from the truth.

The children loved it. For the first time they had the opportunity to run free on a country hillside of their own. Sarah could hear their excited voices calling to one another. In the midst of them was Patrick, louder and more exuberant than all the rest.

Eventually, Patrick came inside to find Sarah sitting on a bench before the fireplace. Her hands were clasped tensely in her lap. She fought desperately to keep the tears from spilling down her cheeks.

Unaware of her feelings, Patrick boomed, "How does it feel to be mistress of a real home again?"

"A real home! This . . . this cabin in the woods isn't even finished!"

For a moment Patrick was surprised into silence.

"It's hardly a cabin in the woods," he said defensively. "We've 1700 acres of cleared land. It is a small plantation, I admit, but it is our own. The house is very new, built especially for you and the children. I . . . I thought you would be happy with it."

Patrick looked so distressed that Sarah hurried across the room and took his hands in hers. She gazed earnestly into his eyes.

"Oh, Patrick, I have always said that I can be happy wherever you and the children are. But really, four rooms for a family of six?"

"There are three rooms down here. That's plenty for us," protested Patrick. "And the attic is huge — perfect for the children. They're young yet!"

"That's just it!" cried Sarah. "They won't be young much longer. Patsy is ten already. She'll be a young lady before we know it."

"Oh," replied Patrick. His shoulders sagged,

and he sighed. "I only meant to make you happy. We've lived so long with your family, I thought . . ."

Sarah's face softened, and she put a finger over her husband's lips.

"You are a marvel in the courtroom, Mr. Henry. But at home you need someone to organize things."

Patrick watched his pretty wife smooth the folds of her dress thoughtfully as she looked about the room in a businesslike manner.

"First, we'll have the walls plastered," she said. "Then we'll see to adding on more rooms. Roundabout does have possibilities."

Patrick grinned at her admiringly. "There's not another woman like you in Virginia!"

Sarah gave him a sidelong glance.

"A pity you did not think to include all thirteen Colonies, Mr. Henry. There's nothing like flattery to soften a woman's heart."

Patrick thought that he was the luckiest man in all thirteen Colonies to have Sarah for a wife. Miraculously she made Roundabout into a comfortable home for them all.

But Patrick soon found that the location of Roundabout Plantation was not very convenient for anything but hunting. His law practice took him away for days and weeks at a time, because it was too far to travel home.

Then eighteen months after his Stamp Act speech, he was again elected to the House of Burgesses, as he was every year after that. Whenever the House met, he was gone more than a month. Patrick returned home only to be called away to the county courthouses. When he had to go to Hanover, he stayed with his father-in-law at Shelton Tavern.

"I don't know what to do," Patrick told John Shelton. "The law doesn't really pay very well. It's difficult for an ordinary man like me to make a substantial living. I want to provide well for my family. That's why I bought Roundabout Plantation. But it's so lonely out there. Sarah doesn't complain, but I don't think she is happy."

"Give her time. She'll get used to it," advised Mr. Shelton. "You've done the wise thing. The wealthiest men in Virginia are plantation owners. Roundabout will add nicely to your income."

"I hope so," said Patrick.

"Oh, a profitable plantation is always a good investment, but the real answer is land. My boy, years ago I bought 3,400 acres in the southwest corner of Virginia for practically nothing at all. That same land is worth a great deal more today. I only wish I could hold onto it longer."

"You're planning to sell?" asked Patrick.

"I have to," admitted John Shelton. "I'm in debt."

"Have you found a buyer?"

"Not yet."

Patrick looked thoughtful. Here was a chance to invest his money in land again. He would not have to live on it or improve it. All he would have to do was wait. Every year Virginia farmers moved to new lands farther and farther west. One day he could sell his land at a profit.

"I would like a chance to look over the land," said Patrick with sudden determination.

Mr. Shelton looked surprised. "It's an expensive proposition, and I shall need all the money I can get."

"I'll borrow what I need," said Patrick. "Will you give me time to investigate?"

Mr. Shelton shrugged. "Why not?" he said. "At least someone in the family might benefit from the investment."

Patrick lost no time in making up a party to investigate the land. He called upon his brother

William, who now was a prosperous plantation owner himself.

"I would appreciate your opinion, Will," said Patrick.

Will grinned. "I haven't been on a good hunting trip in a coon's age, Patrick. When do we leave?"

The land was along a river deep within the wilds of Virginia's western lands.

"Good farmland," pronounced William. "And far enough away for a hothead like you to hide if the Governor orders you seized and brought to England for trial. All you have to worry about here are Indians."

Will was joking, but Patrick knew that recent events in England were not encouraging. In June of 1767, Parliament had passed the Townshend Acts. There were new taxes on tea, paper, window glass, and other items. Massachusetts began a boycott on these items. The people refused to buy them rather than pay the tax. Virginia supported Massachusetts.

Some of the members of Parliament were furious. They revived an old law. Under it patriots such as Samuel Adams, John Hancock, and Patrick Henry could be arrested and taken to England.

"Well, it's always best to be prepared," Patrick told his brother calmly.

On Will's advice, Patrick bought the land. Not long afterward he moved his entire family back to Hanover. He left his overseer in charge of the plantation.

Sarah seemed to change overnight. Her step became light, and she sang as she went about her work.

"Patrick, I don't mind telling you now. I could not have stood it another month. I was so lonesome!"

"The next home we buy will be nearer civilization," said Patrick. Even as he said it, he hoped that he could keep that promise.

When the House of Burgesses met in May of 1769, Thomas Jefferson began to serve his first term as a representative from Albemarle County.

"You have another ally, Patrick, if you need me."

"Virginia needs you, Thomas," said Patrick.

Virginia had a new governor appointed by the King. At first Lord Botetourt got along very well with the people of Virginia. But the colonists were furious about the Townshend Acts. It was not long

before the popular young governor found himself
in conflict with the people.

"Another tax! Another tax without consulting
the Colonies! Will Parliament never understand
that we must have our rights as free Englishmen?"
cried the people.

The governors had been ordered by England
not to allow the local government to act against the
new tax laws this time. One after another, the general
assemblies were dissolved as they tried to protest
the laws. The Burgesses decided to vote on
their resolutions against the tax before the Governor
knew what they were doing.

When the House of Burgesses met, they went
into closed session.

"Lock the doors," commanded the Speaker.

The order was carried out just in time. A messenger
from the Governor had to wait outside with
the news that Governor Botetourt was expecting
the members in the council chamber.

The House then had time to vote on a series of
resolutions. They voted to strengthen their boycott
against the taxed items. They protested the law
that would seize the colonists and carry them off to
England for trial. Then they unlocked the doors
and let the messenger in.

"Now we can go to see the Governor. He's waited long enough," Patrick told Thomas and winked.

The members of the House of Burgesses climbed the stairs to the council chamber. Patrick and Thomas stood with the others while the Governor dissolved the House.

"He treats us like children who have been naughty," said Richard Henry Lee.

"But we are not children," said Patrick. "Come, shall we join our friends?"

Led by Patrick and some of the younger members, the Burgesses met again in a large room at nearby Raleigh Tavern. This time it was not Patrick who made the next move.

Seldom did the master of Mount Vernon rise to speak. But today the tall, regal figure stood before them.

"Mr. Chairman," said Colonel George Washington, "I have here a detailed series of resolutions for consideration. And I propose that we plan an even wider boycott of British goods unless the Townshend Acts are repealed within three months."

Patrick spoke eloquently in support of the proposal. When it was passed, he was the first to sign the boycott agreements. He did so with a flourish.

Later William chided his brother. "You'll be in need of that new land of yours sooner than you think."

Patrick only laughed.

"Nonsense, Will, the boycott will be a success."

"I hope for your sake, it is. They say the King's justice can reach to the ends of the earth."

"The King's men have never been tested on the Virginia frontier," answered Patrick. "I'm not worried."

Trade between Britain and the Colonies declined rapidly. By March, 1770, England had lost so much money that the Townshend duties were repealed — all but the tax on tea. At first, no one realized what a serious problem that would cause.

8

"I Am an American"

At home in Hanover, Patrick Henry had an announcement. He gathered Sarah and the children about him, holding the baby in his lap.

"Mr. Robert Carter Nicholas asked me to call on him while I was in Williamsburg."

"Did he?" said Sarah, hardly glancing up from her sewing.

Now that they were back in town, she was constantly busy, seeing to it that she and the children were appropriately dressed. She gazed at her husband's worn black suit unhappily. If only Patrick cared more about his clothes. He hadn't got a new suit in years.

"Calling on Mr. Nicholas wasn't unusual, was it, Papa? You often do that, don't you?" asked Patsy.

"Yes," said Patrick, "but what he had to say this time was unusual. His duties as treasurer of the colony keep him so busy that he is forced to give up his law practice."

"He's a wealthy man," said young John knowingly. "He can afford it."

"He's a wealthy man and a brilliant lawyer," said Patrick. "His practice in the General Court in Williamsburg is worth a small fortune. He has offered that practice to me."

Sarah let her sewing fall from her hands. Patsy stopped fussing with little Anne's ribbons. John and William simply stared. Patrick enjoyed their surprise.

" 'Well, now, Mr. Nicholas,' I said. 'Are you certain you mean to make this offer to me? You may recall that barely ten years ago you refused to sign my license to practice law. You found my background wanting then.' "

Sarah caught her breath. "Patrick! How could you speak to the honorable Mr. Nicholas like that after he paid you such a compliment!"

"I couldn't," said Patrick innocently. "And I didn't. I merely accepted with all due graciousness."

"Oh, Papa!" cried Patsy, rushing to hug him and nearly knocking off his brown wig.

Patrick sighed. "Careful, young lady," he

warned, straightening his wig. "Would you reveal the most closely guarded secret in all Virginia?"

Patsy gazed at her father curiously. "What do you mean?"

"That Patrick Henry is rapidly losing his hair!"

Practicing law before the General Court took Patrick to Williamsburg four times a year in addition to the times when the House of Burgesses met. But the fees for cases before the higher court were quite substantial and worth the extra traveling. With Mr. Nicholas' clients, as well as with his own, Patrick was able to provide rather well for his family. Not long afterward he made another announcement.

"I've a rather large surprise for everyone," he said.

"Do you have it with you, Papa?" asked William, who loved surprises.

"No," said Patrick. "But it is in Hanover County."

"A new home!" cried Patsy hopefully.

Patsy was fifteen and very pretty. Already young men were beginning to call. She was especially fond of a distant cousin, John Fontaine. It would be wonderful to have a place of their own for entertaining.

"How did you guess?" asked Patrick. He walked briskly across the room to Sarah. "This time there is ample room, my dear. There are seventeen rooms, counting the attic. The walls in the main chambers are paneled in walnut wood. It's a home we can be proud of."

"Where is this marvel?" asked Sarah, hardly daring to believe their good fortune.

"Not far from my parents' home at Mount Brilliant. I've purchased Scotchtown."

"Scotchtown!" echoed Sarah.

It was one of the largest plantations in Hanover, but there was a tragic story connected with it, which made many people feel that it was an unlucky place. The previous owner, Mr. Chiswell, had died under very sad circumstances. In an argument he had killed another man. Later, fearing punishment, he had taken his own life.

Sarah had an uncomfortable and an unreasonable feeling of foreboding. But she refused to let such foolishness spoil her family's happiness. Patrick Henry was now a wealthy lawyer. People would expect him to own a country estate. If only he had chosen another plantation! Sarah could not help feeling that she would never be happy there.

A few weeks later, satisfied that his family was

comfortable in the new home, Patrick found himself caught up in public affairs once again. After
only two years in office, Governor Botetourt died.
Although some of his actions had been unpopular,
the young governor had gotten along well with the
colonists. After the Townshend taxes had been repealed as a result of the boycotts, the Colonies enjoyed a peaceful and prosperous period. There
were some isolated incidents of trouble. England
still tried to enforce the trade laws, which limited
the buying and selling of goods between the Colonies and other countries. Although referred to in-
correctly as a massacre, there was a small riot in
Boston, in which five colonists were killed.

Then in 1771, Lord Dunmore was appointed as
the new governor of Virginia. He was a poor
choice, for he did not get on well with the people.

Feeling that he could make all necessary deci-
sions without them, he did not call for a meeting of
the House of Burgesses until 1773. When the
House did meet, the Governor dismissed them
quickly.

"We have pressing problems to discuss," protested Richard Henry Lee. "What of the rumors
we have heard from New England?"

Recently, colonists in Rhode Island had been

responsible for burning a Royal ship. Rumors reached Virginia that the guilty men were being deprived of their legal rights as British citizens.

Several of the leaders, including Patrick, met once again at the Raleigh Tavern.

"Rumors can be dangerous. What we need are facts," said Patrick Henry. "We must establish some method of rapid communication among the Colonies."

"If every colony appointed a permanent Committee of Correspondence, we could easily keep well informed. The committee could send out newsletters to all the Colonies," suggested Thomas Jefferson.

The idea was quickly adopted in Virginia. Soon almost all the Colonies had such committees. Patrick and Thomas worked closely on the correspondence for Virginia.

Patrick was so busy in Williamsburg that he hardly had time to return home for any long period of time. When Sarah told him that Patsy wanted to marry John Fontaine, he was amazed.

"She's a child!" he cried.

"She's nineteen," said Sarah. "I was younger than that when we married."

"Nineteen and married!" cried Patrick, still

looking bewildered and hurt.

Sarah laughed. "Don't worry. We won't lose Patsy entirely. She and John plan to live nearby. We'll see them often."

Patrick finally accepted the idea. He enjoyed the wedding thoroughly. He had a fine family, and he was proud of all his children. There was even a new baby at Scotchtown, another son. Sarah called him Edward.

"Six fine children! Patsy is happily married. We have a comfortable home. Sarah, we are indeed fortunate!" said Patrick.

He did not notice how tired Sarah looked. He was home so seldom that he did not know that she spent more and more time in her room. Finally, Patsy took her father aside.

"Mother never complains," she said. "But I think she is very ill."

Patrick refused to believe this. "It's natural for her to be a little tired. She has the responsibility of this large home and the new baby."

"No, Papa! It's more than that. Even the doctor says so. He's coming to speak with you later today."

Alarmed, Patrick spent the morning with

Sarah. She seemed to have a fever. Most of the time she did not know him at all.

When the doctor finally arrived, Patrick grasped his arm insistently.

"You must do something," he cried.

The doctor shook his head sadly.

"I wish there were something I could do."

"But surely there is a cure. In time Sarah will be well again."

"I'm afraid not, Mr. Henry. I'm so sorry."

Patrick hired a special nurse to give his wife constant care. It soon became obvious that the doctor was right. Sarah seldom knew who she was, nor did she recognize members of her family. Patrick was heartbroken.

Patsy began to worry about her father as well. No longer did the house ring with his laughter. When he smiled at all, it was with a sad, faraway look in his eyes.

When his work called him to Williamsburg, he went reluctantly, leaving Patsy in charge. Through the Committee of Correspondence, news of the Boston Tea Party on December 16, 1773, spread throughout the Colonies.

Three hundred forty-two chests of tea were

thrown from the ships into Boston Harbor. The colonists had been told to unload the tea, but they did not want to buy it and pay the hated tea tax. This was their reply.

"Don't pay the tax! Don't buy the tea!" the Committee of Correspondence advised the other colonists.

There were ships carrying tea in many colonial harbors. Soon there were other "tea parties." Simply furious with this outrageous action, the King ordered the port of Boston closed on June 1, 1774.

"We cannot sit back and watch while the King destroys the liberty of a sister colony," George Washington told the Burgesses.

"A protest may mean more trouble for us all," said a more conservative member.

"On the day the port is closed, let the Colonies declare a day of prayer and fasting to turn the King's heart to justice," suggested Thomas Jefferson. "That will show England how strongly we feel."

"And how could it cause any real trouble? Who can object to prayer?" asked Patrick.

Although Governor Dunmore had dissolved the House of Burgesses again because he did not

approve of their actions, the men met at Raleigh
Tavern. They passed the resolutions there. Soon
everyone in the Colonies heard about the day of
prayer through the Committees of Correspondence.

The day of prayer served to unite the men of
Virginia. Governor Dunmore looked on in angry
silence. There was nothing he could do about it.

"One day of prayer will not open the port of
Boston," said Peyton Randolph. "All the Colonies
must act together to preserve the rights of each."

"What do you propose, sir?" asked Patrick.

It was surprising how many of the older, conservative members had come around to a more
revolutionary way of thinking, thought Patrick. He
remembered how hopefully he had awaited the
action of one of the older leaders upon the Stamp
Act. Now they needed little urging.

"I propose that we call an intercolonial meeting. We must decide upon a plan together."

Patrick Henry, along with Peyton Randolph,
George Washington, and Richard Henry Lee were
three of the delegates who would represent Virginia at the meeting in Philadelphia.

Patrick knew that he would have to be away
from home for some time. When he returned to

Scotchtown, he found Sarah worse than ever. Patrick's mother had come from Jane and Samuel Meredith's home to help Patsy with the family. Mrs. Henry had been living with her daughter since Patrick's father had died.

"I am afraid Sarah will not live much longer," said Mrs. Henry.

Patrick buried his face in his hands. He could not bear to think of losing Sarah. They had been so happy together.

"I'll send a message to Williamsburg. Someone else can take my place at the Congress," he said.

"No, Papa," said Patsy. "There is nothing that you can do here. Everyone in Virginia is counting on you. You must go."

In the end, Patrick agreed and traveled to Pennsylvania. Philadelphia was much bigger than Williamsburg. It was even then a busy port city on the Delaware River. The streets of the marketplace were crowded with visitors from all over the world.

Slowly the delegates gathered. On September 5 they met in Carpenters' Hall. Peyton Randolph was elected chairman, and then the delegates set about the work of organizing the meeting.

At first no one quite knew where to begin. They talked about the place of small colonies and about the number of votes they should have in relation to large colonies.

Patrick spoke briefly on the opening day. Many of the delegates did not realize who he was. Certainly this pale gentleman in the dark parson's clothes was not recognized as the famous Patrick Henry, author of the Stamp Act speech. He looked thin and tired, hardly capable of making a fiery speech.

Soon it became apparent that the delegates would not accomplish anything if they quarreled among themselves. The problem of assigning votes to large and small colonies threatened to defeat them. Finally, Patrick rose to speak on this subject. His shoulders were stooped, and he looked much smaller than his six feet.

As usual, Patrick began quietly. As he developed his ideas, his voice grew firm and deep. The delegates began to whisper among themselves.

"It really is Patrick Henry! Who would have thought he looked like that?"

"Gentlemen, this meeting may only be the first of its kind," said Patrick.

He asked the delegates to set aside all petty differences. He asked them to think of themselves as one united group. He insisted on his point.

"Gentlemen, I am not a Virginian, but an American," he announced in his full, rich voice.

An American! It was the first time that anyone had said such a thing in the Colonies. Moved by Patrick's plea, the delegates began to think of themselves as Americans. They acted together for the good of all. At the end of that session many of the men congratulated Patrick on his speech.

"It was a good beginning, Mr. Henry," said John Adams of Boston. "But it is only the beginning. I fear we have a long, hard way to go as Americans."

Patrick knew that Mr. Adams meant war. But no one else was ready to think of that yet.

9

"Give Me Liberty"

Fall at Scotchtown was a lovely time. In the cooler weather the hillsides glowed with brilliant color. If only Sarah could enjoy it! But she was too ill even to leave her room.

Patrick busied himself with the affairs of his plantation. He took his older boys, John and William, hunting. He spent long hours just sitting beside Sarah, hoping that for perhaps a moment she would open her eyes and recognize him. But she never did.

The children were considerate of their mother. About the house they were quiet. They played their noisiest games far from the windows. One day Patrick came upon three-year-old Edward marching up and down, a long stick against his shoulder.

"Here, what's this?" asked Patrick, lifting him high into the air.

Neddy was so startled he dropped his play-gun.

"Put me down! Put me down!" squealed the boy. "I'm a soldier!"

Slowly, Patrick put the little boy down. He looked long into the child's serious, flushed face and thought he did see a soldier there. Impulsively, Patrick hugged his son hard.

He's only a baby, he thought. But John will go and William, too, if war comes.

Two of his sons might have to risk the dangers of battle. Was this the price of freedom? Patrick knew it might very well be. There were tears in his eyes when he rose and walked back to the house.

The First Continental Congress had sent a protest to the King. It was a Declaration of Rights and Grievances. If the King chose to ignore this message, the Colonies threatened a boycott on all British goods. If an agreement could not be reached, the Colonies would have to fight.

Already Massachusetts had armed and had trained militia. This small group of farmers and merchants lived at home and went about their work. But they could be ready at a moment's notice, and so they had earned the name Minutemen. Patrick was convinced that Virginia must do the same.

Five months after the First Continental Congress had met, the King had still done nothing about the colonists' demands. British troops occupied Boston. The time had come for action. March 20, 1775, was the date of the Second Virginia Convention. New delegates to the Philadelphia Convention would be elected.

"They can't hold the Convention in Williamsburg this time," John Syme told his half brother Patrick. "I'm afraid Governor Dunmore would move against us, arrest our leaders, and put them all on a ship for London."

"You don't really think he would get away with something like that," said Patrick. "It would be the quickest road to war."

"True, but the Governor is just foolish enough to make such a move. Your life, Patrick, and the lives of all our leaders would be in danger."

It was decided to hold the Convention in the small town of Richmond for safety's sake. St. John's Church was the only place large enough for the meeting.

For three days the men of Virginia argued and got nowhere. Then Patrick Henry, certain that drastic measures were needed, offered three resolutions:

1. That it is not necessary for England to
   keep troops in the Colonies, since the
   Colonies can defend themselves very well.
2. That the establishment of a militia *now* is
   necessary to secure the rights and liberties of the colonists.
3. That a committee be established to prepare the defense of Virginia.

To Patrick's surprise many of his old friends
bitterly opposed these resolutions.

"It's too soon for such action," said Richard
Bland.

"You'll lead us into war," argued Robert Carter
Nicholas. "We must go slowly. Wait and see, Mr.
Henry. Wait and see. We can hope the King might
yet have a change of heart."

But Patrick Henry thought that the Colonies
had waited long enough. He rose to make the most
magnificent speech of his career.

"There is no longer room for hope," he said. "If
we wish to be free, . . . we must fight."

Patrick straightened to his full height. He held
out his arms.

"Why stand we here idle? What is it the gentlemen wish? What would they have . . . ? Men cry
peace, peace, and there is no peace."

Patrick lowered his head and held his hands before him as though he were a slave in chains.

"Is life so dear, or peace so sweet, as to be purchased at the price of chains and slavery? Forbid it, Almighty God!" he cried.

Looking about the room, Patrick paused. There was not a sound.

"I know not what course others may take, but as for me, give me liberty," he cried.

Holding an ivory letter opener as he would a knife, he paused. His voice grew husky.

"Or give me death!"

The Convention was stunned. Patrick's thundering tones carried to those people who waited anxiously outside.

Suddenly the wooden rafters shook with cheers and applause. The Convention voted to arm. Where courage was necessary, Virginians were never wanting. Once again, Patrick Henry's magnificent power as a speaker had moved men to action.

Patrick was appointed to the Committee of Safety, along with George Washington and Thomas Jefferson. He was also named again as a delegate to the Second Continental Congress.

When word reached the British governor that

Virginia had voted to arm its men, he became uneasy. In Massachusetts, General Gage marched his troops to Concord, where he expected to take away the colonial guns and ammunition. He was met by Minutemen. Shots were exchanged, and some Americans were killed. On the way back to Boston, many British soldiers lost their lives as angry colonists shot at the retreating men.

On April 20, 1775, Governor Dunmore ordered guns and powder removed from the Powder Magazine in Williamsburg. The soldiers acted at midnight. He did not want a repetition of General Gage's disaster. Before the colonists knew what had happened, the arms were carried to a British ship in the James River. There the Virginians could not get them.

Patrick knew very well that the next step the Governor might take would be to arrest such leaders as Thomas Jefferson, George Washington, and himself. Unless something was done at once, no one was safe.

Colonel Washington organized a group of men at Fredericksburg. They were ready to march on the capital at Williamsburg. At the last minute they received word from Peyton Randolph that the affair was being settled satisfactorily. The men

went home without waiting to hear that a settlement had not actually been made. Word came to Patrick that it was not settled at all.

As a member of the Committee of Safety he acted at once.

"It will take Colonel Washington too long to reorganize his men," Patrick told his son-in-law, John Fontaine. "It is up to us to act now. I want you to get a message to the men of Hanover County."

The message asked the men to meet at New Castle, Virginia, on May second.

"We must discuss business of the highest importance to American liberty."

Over one hundred fifty armed volunteers met with Patrick Henry on the appointed day.

"When men are deprived of their weapons, they lose the ability to defend themselves," Patrick told the men. "We must recapture the guns and powder or force Governor Dunmore to pay us the three hundred thirty pounds they are worth. We must march on Williamsburg, if necessary."

The men agreed. With Patrick leading them, they moved toward Williamsburg. Governor Dunmore knew that he was in no position to fight the Virginians. Outside the city the men were met by a messenger. He turned over the money to Patrick.

Triumphantly the men returned to their homes, satisfied that they had taught the Governor a lesson. But Governor Dunmore had the last word. He issued a warrant for the arrest of Patrick Henry!

"Papa," cried Patsy. "You must hide."

"Nonsense, my dear. I am as safe in my own home as I can be anywhere. We're surrounded by patriots who would fight to protect me."

"But soon you will be going to Philadelphia for the Congress. Who will protect you then?"

On May eleventh, Patsy had her answer. A group of armed men arrived early in the morning.

"We've come to escort Mr. Henry," they told Patsy.

"There you are," grinned Patrick. "I couldn't be safer."

The delegates to the Second Continental Congress went about their business quickly. If war came, they must be ready. They chose George Washington to be Commander in Chief.

"I fear, gentlemen, that I cannot accept without giving the matter some thought. I would like to give you my decision tomorrow."

No one expected Colonel Washington to refuse, and yet the delegates were worried. Colonel Washington was such a modest man!

The next day he accepted, but he confided to Patrick that he felt he did not have enough experience for such an important position.

"My reputation will decline from this day forward," he said sadly.

"Not at all," said Patrick. "From this day on, the world will learn of your great abilities."

Most of the delegates were still reluctant to fight.

"Let us send one more petition to the King," said John Dickinson, a farmer from Pennsylvania. "Let us beg him once more to restore harmony."

Patrick Henry did not think that another petition would do any good. Benjamin Franklin, who had returned from his post representing the Colonies in England, agreed with Patrick.

"I fear that Britain will not have sense enough to accept this last opportunity, but I am not against it," said Mr. Franklin.

In Virginia, the Convention was meeting that summer to organize an army. Patrick Henry was appointed Colonel of the First Regiment.

With the work of the Philadelphia Congress over for a few weeks, Patrick returned to Virginia to find that he was now not only an outlaw but a soldier.

10

Difficult Tasks

The grounds of the College of William and Mary became a camp for Virginia's First Regiment under Colonel Patrick Henry in the autumn of 1775. Supplies were short, and the volunteers were asked to bring their own squirrel guns. Most of the men slept in the open. Tents were promised soon. But winter came, and many of the men still slept under the stars.

The volunteer soldiers were devoted to their military leader. No problem was too small for them to bring to him. He always listened sympathetically.

"My wife is sick, sir," a young sergeant told the Colonel.

They were sitting before a campfire, trying to warm themselves.

"I . . . I want to serve, sir, you understand. But I can't help worrying about her."

"How long have you been married, Sergeant?" inquired Patrick kindly.

"Fourteen months, sir."

"Ah! Any children?"

"We're expecting our first, but Anne's so sick." The young soldier turned away to hide his tears.

Patrick reached out and patted the boy's trembling shoulder.

"My wife was sick for a long time. I know how you feel, Sergeant. You had better go to her."

The boy stared at his commanding officer.

"You mean desert, sir?"

"No, no!" said Patrick. "You'll be coming back, won't you?"

"Oh, yes, sir!" promised the boy.

"Then go!"

The Sergeant rose. "How . . . how is your wife now, sir?"

Patrick hesitated. When he spoke, his voice was low.

"She died a few months ago."

As Colonel Henry turned away to stare into the fire, the Sergeant could almost feel his loneliness.

Patrick's method of handling soldiers lacked the strict military discipline expected of an army officer. The Committee of Safety was worried.

"Patrick Henry is not a military man," complained Chairman Edmund Pendleton. "From the reports I have, he's too lax with the men."

"The Convention voted him Commander in Chief of Virginia forces," said Richard Henry Lee. "There's nothing we can do about that."

"Mr. Henry is a very popular man," said Chairman Pendleton. "That's why he was appointed. He is a fine political leader, but he is not a soldier."

Neither the chairman nor any of the committee members knew how to tell Patrick that he would serve the people better at the Convention, planning their course of action.

When Governor Dunmore left Williamsburg, he took possession of the city of Norfolk at the mouth of Chesapeake Bay. From there he was able to cut off any supplies to Williamsburg that came from the sea.

"We must send a force to take Norfolk from the British," said Edmund Pendleton. "I'm afraid that Mr. Henry has no experience for such an important task. I propose to send Colonel Woodford with the Second Regiment."

When news of this assignment reached Patrick, he was angry.

"Am I, or am I not, Commander in Chief of Virginia forces?" he demanded in a letter to the Committee of Safety.

It soon became obvious that the Committee had little confidence in him. Patrick was hurt. He felt that he had not been given a fair chance. He did not know that even General Washington felt that Patrick's new assignment was a "capital mistake." Finally, very discouraged, Patrick Henry resigned his military position.

The men of the First Regiment were furious.

"If we don't serve under Patrick Henry, we won't serve under anyone," they cried.

Many threatened to leave at once. Patrick spent one more night in camp talking to the men individually and in small groups. He convinced them to stay. At least he had the satisfaction of knowing that his men supported him.

Patrick returned to Scotchtown in time to supervise spring planting. In May he returned to Williamsburg for the Fourth Virginia Convention.

Many colonists had been reading a pamphlet called *Common Sense,* by a young man named Thomas Paine.

"The colonists must move forward," said Mr. Paine. "And they will move forward if they have an important goal. Independence is that goal."

The Convention voted to have its delegates in Philadelphia offer a motion for independence.

"I, too, wish independence for the Colonies," argued Patrick Henry. "But first, I feel we should approach France for help. Alone, I think we would have little chance against the British."

The overwhelming feeling was for independence now. Patrick did not oppose it.

That day the British flag was taken down from the Capitol. Virginia already thought of herself as free!

The Convention went about the business of setting up a plan of government. Thomas Jefferson was one of the delegates who rode to Philadelphia. That June he was chosen to draft the Declaration of Independence. In Virginia, Patrick Henry was elected the first American governor.

"Papa, what will you wear for the ceremonies?" asked Patsy.

"Wear? Why, I hadn't thought about it."

"But you should, Papa. Your old suit would not be appropriate for such an occasion. Mama would have liked to see you in something splendid."

Patrick bowed his head. How pleased Sarah

would have been to see this day! Patsy was right. Sarah would have wanted him to look the part of a governor.

On July 4, 1776, independence was officially proclaimed. The next day Patrick Henry was sworn in as Governor of Virginia. He wore a scarlet cloak and a new black suit. His stockings were silk, and his shoes had wide silver buckles.

"Papa, you look magnificent," Patsy told him just before the ceremonies.

"Mr. Henry is a very handsome man," said Patsy's friend, Dorothea Dandridge.

Dolly had grown into a beautiful young woman. Patrick could hardly believe that she was the little girl who had enjoyed his stories so long ago.

Patrick bowed. "Thank you, ladies. I consider those great compliments because they come from young women of fine taste. Had you said anything else I would have been disappointed in you," he said, his blue eyes twinkling.

"Oh, Papa, when will you stop teasing?" asked Patsy. "It isn't seemly, for the Governor, I mean."

She pretended annoyance. Actually, Patsy was pleased to have her father acting like his old self again. It had been a long time since she had seen him in such high spirits.

"I think it is charming," said Dorothea, tossing her shining black curls and looking directly into the new governor's eyes.

The ceremonies were long, and the day was hot. For some unaccountable reason, Governor Henry found himself shivering. A few days later, he was in bed with a high fever.

"It's malaria," said the doctor. "Williamsburg's damp climate is the worst thing for the disease. I advise you to retire to Scotchtown until you are better."

The new governor was too ill to argue. His sister, Anne Christian, and Patsy made all the arrangements. They left the Governor's Mansion and went home. In the fall they returned to Williamsburg.

"It's too soon," warned the doctor.

"There is much for me to do," insisted Governor Henry. "We are at war."

Only a month later Governor Henry was at Scotchtown again. He was too sick to carry on his duties.

Patsy cared for her father. She insisted that this time he must follow the doctor's orders.

"And I will be here to see that you do, Governor Henry," said Dorothea.

True to her word, she visited often. Patrick found that he enjoyed the company of this lively, intelligent young woman.

One day Patsy brought a visitor to see her father. He was a young man, wearing buckskins, who looked as though he had been on a long hunting trip.

"I'm George Rogers Clark, sir, from Kentucky," he introduced himself.

"Kentucky!" Patrick sighed. The word was like music.

"When I think of Kentucky Territory, I remember the wonderful hunting and fishing trips I've had in the wilderness. It must be a splendid place to live."

"It's a dangerous one now. I've been appointed head of the militia by the settlers," said Mr. Clark. "We're plagued by Indian attacks inspired by the British."

"How can I help?" asked Governor Henry.

"I think we can help each other," said Mr. Clark. "We need guns and powder to hold off the British and the Indians. We will not only defend ourselves, but we will protect Virginia from an attack on the western frontier."

Patrick felt that George Rogers Clark was right.

He wrote a letter to his executive council asking them to support Mr. Clark's plan. It was this decision that saved Virginia from disastrous Indian attacks on the western boundaries.

After four months of rest, Governor Henry returned to his duties in Williamsburg. While battles raged in the north, Virginia, under Governor Henry's direction, began to build up a small navy. These ships slipped through the British blockade to trade with the Spanish and the French in the West Indies. There they obtained important supplies for the Colonies.

At the end of his first year in office, Patrick Henry was elected for a second time.

"You must be very proud, Governor Henry. Virginia has great confidence in you," Dorothea said.

"It's more like a feeling of relief," said Patrick.

Dorothea looked startled. Patrick hid a smile.

"Virginia could not see me as a military leader. It's nice to know they think I'm good for something."

"You are too modest, sir," answered Dolly. "You are very much admired by everyone. I am sure that most Virginians would feel you were capable of filling almost any position."

Patrick grinned mischievously.

"And how would Miss Dorothea Dandridge look upon me as a husband? Is that a position I could fill?"

Dolly looked up through her long, dark lashes. "Easily," she said.

They were married a short time later. Everyone was happy for the Governor and his young bride. The children were delighted with their new mother. But there was little time for celebration. Not long afterward a messenger brought terrifying news.

"General Howe is in Chesapeake Bay with a fleet of warships."

Governor Henry looked grim. "The British must be stopped," he announced.

Privately, he wondered whether this were possible. The British forces completely outnumbered those of Virginia.

11

A Narrow Escape

Dolly lifted her chin stubbornly. "If you stay in Williamsburg, we shall stay with you."

Patrick shook his head. "You don't understand, my dear," he said. "General Howe and his troops are only twenty miles away. There is no reason for you and the children to risk arrest and humiliation. If you leave now, you can be safe at Leatherwood. It would greatly relieve my mind to know that you were out of danger."

Patrick had sold Scotchtown, which had held so many sad memories. Two hundred miles inland, in the newly created Henry County, he had purchased Leatherwood, another plantation.

Dolly's dark eyes flashed. "And what of your own danger? The British would find the arrest of the Governor a great advantage. Surely you plan to leave the city in time to avoid capture."

"Of course," said Patrick. "But . . ."

"No, sir, my mind is firm. Unless you order me to go, and I hope you will not, I intend to face all the challenges of life at my husband's side."

Patrick sighed and then smiled. He knew that further argument was useless. He could not help being proud of his young wife's courage.

"Very well, my dear. As you wish. But what would the people of Virginia think if they knew that the Governor was not master in his own house?"

Dolly raised innocent eyes to his. "Your secret, sir, is safe with me."

Patrick laughed aloud, offered his arm, and together they joined the children for tea.

General Howe, it seemed, was not interested in Virginia. He sailed to the headwaters of Chesapeake Bay and marched north with his troops to Philadelphia. There he remained during the winter of 1777-78 and enjoyed the hospitality of the Loyalists. General Washington, on the other hand, spent the long, cold months at Valley Forge, with hardly enough food or clothing to keep his troops together.

Early in the year Governor Henry received another visit from George Rogers Clark. No longer did Colonel Clark wear buckskins. He was dressed in the uniform of a Continental soldier.

"Are things quiet in Kentucky, Colonel?" asked Governor Henry.

"Kentucky is quieter than most places, thanks to you, sir. The British are inciting the Indians to attack settlers as far north as New York. Men, women, and children are mercilessly murdered and their scalps taken for the 'hair buyers,' as the British are called."

"What do you suggest?"

"I propose to lead my men against the British forts in the wilderness. My people know how to approach the Indians. We speak their language. We can win them over and capture the British forts, perhaps even Detroit. But we need guns and ammunition."

Once again Patrick was impressed by this brave woodsman. The British counted on the support of the Indians. It would be a serious blow if the tribes turned against them. Patrick recommended that the House of Delegates give Colonel Clark the supplies he needed.

That summer he was able to announce that the Colonel's mission had been a great success. Al-

though there were not enough men and ammunition to take Detroit, the forts, Kaskaskia, Vincennes, and Cahokia were captured.

In June of 1778, Governor Henry was elected for a third term. Dolly was almost disappointed by her husband's popularity. He worked long hours, and she worried about his health.

"You must rest, or you will make yourself ill again," she warned.

"There is no time to rest," insisted Patrick. "Only one more year," he promised.

Dolly knew that Patrick would be forced to retire at the end of a third term. The Virginia Convention had limited the governorship to three consecutive terms. She looked forward to the time when the entire family could retire to Leatherwood. But in the spring of 1779, she became alarmed by the plans of some members of the House of Delegates.

"Governor Henry has really had two official terms," they argued. "He was only elected by the House of Delegates twice. It was the Virginia Convention that elected him the first time."

Patrick did not agree with this argument, and he planned to retire to his home. Still, there were some people who did not know this. Once Patrick's half brother John Syme was stopped on the street.

"The day Patrick Henry declares himself dictator . . . ," the man began angrily.

"Dictator!" echoed John in astonishment. "I can
assure you, sir, my brother has no such intention."

But the man shook his head knowingly. "On
that day," he continued, "he will feel my dagger in
his heart."

John indignantly reported this conversation to
Patrick. The Governor only shook his head.

"A man in public office is bound to make enemies, John. As long as these do not outnumber his
friends, he is safe."

Thomas Jefferson was elected the second Governor of Virginia. Soon afterward, Patrick, Dolly,
and the children retired to their new home at
Leatherwood. It was fortunate that now there was
time for rest. No sooner did they arrive, however,
than Patrick came down with fever again.

When news reached the Henrys that Patrick
had been elected to the Philadelphia Congress, he
was too ill to accept. While Patrick was recovering,
Governor Jefferson wrote him a long letter begging
him to return to public life. "We have great need
of your inspiration," he said.

The war was not going well for the Americans. But there was added hope when the French entered the battle. Marquis de Lafayette came to aid General Washington. Patrick thought from the beginning that the colonists should have awaited help from France. Now he thought victory could only be a matter of time. Soon Spain and Holland turned against England, too.

In May of 1780, Patrick was elected to the House of Delegates from Henry County. The Capital had been moved to Richmond. Williamsburg was no longer safe. By January 1781, Patrick proposed that not even Richmond would be free of attack. The Capital must move again.

In March the British, led by the traitor, Benedict Arnold, were moving up the James River. Lord Cornwallis was marching north from the Carolinas.

"Gentlemen, we must send an urgent plea to Congress for men and supplies," Patrick urged.

Congress responded at once, but they were almost too late. General Arnold burned Richmond, and Lord Cornwallis sent Colonel Tarleton and his raiders to terrorize the countryside.

Governor Jefferson had retreated to his home at Monticello. The legislature was meeting at

Charlottesville, only a few miles away. Word reached the delegates that Colonel Tarleton was coming.

"Tarleton rode his horse right up the front steps of Scotchtown and on into the main hall," reported a messenger. "Thinking Mr. Henry still lived there, the Colonel demanded his arrest."

"It is fortunate for me that British intelligence is somewhat behind the times," said Patrick.

Colonel Tarleton's raids were no laughing matter. He struck often at night, rousing citizens from their beds. He arrested some and killed others.

"We must leave Charlottesville at once," Patrick told the delegates. "The government cannot operate if we are captured. This is just what the British want."

Patrick Henry, Benjamin Harrison, Colonel William Christian, and John Tyler hurried off on horseback, hoping to reach home and safety. They stopped the first night at an inn. No one knew where the raiders were. It would not do to be found camping in the open. They needed a place to hide. But the woman who ran the inn would have nothing to do with them.

"Who are you?" she demanded, peering at them suspiciously.

"We're from the House of Delegates. We've been meeting in Charlottesville. Word has reached us that Colonel Tarleton is on his way," explained Patrick.

To his surprise, the woman began to shout. "Cowards! You ran from Charlottesville! My husband has gone there to defend you!"

"You would not want the British to capture the men of the Virginia government," protested Patrick. "Here is Chairman Harrison himself," he added, indicating one of his companions.

"What? I've always thought well of Chairman Harrison. Now I know he is a coward."

The woman moved to close and bolt the door, but Patrick stopped her. He must find a way to convince this woman to help them.

"Look here, madam, these men are John Tyler and Colonel Christian. Surely you cannot think they would leave the city unless there was good reason to do so."

The woman's eyes narrowed, and her lips curled in disdain. "Cowards! All of you!"

John Tyler stepped forward. "Madam, you are,

I trust, familiar with the name of Patrick Henry."

The old woman's eyes glowed. "Ah, Patrick Henry," she cried. "If you were like Patrick Henry, you would never run from the enemy."

"But, madam," said Patrick. "I am Patrick Henry. And I tell you, it was necessary for us to leave."

The woman's eyes grew wide. She threw open the door. "Forgive me. I did not know. If you say so, Mr. Henry, it must be all right."

Sighing with relief, the men entered the inn.

John Tyler laughed nervously. "They say Patrick Henry's voice can charm beasts. I did not know his name would open doors."

"Neither did I," said Patrick. "But I'm grateful for the privilege. That was a near thing, Mr. Tyler, a near thing."

The men refreshed themselves with good food and rest. The next day they rode off, leaving Tarleton's raiders far behind.

The war continued, and much of the fighting went on in Virginia. British troops were forced back and onto a peninsula. There, on October 19, 1781, surrounded by the Americans and the French, General Cornwallis surrendered. The war

was over, and the Colonies were truly independent at last.

After the war, many Americans had bitter feelings for those who had remained loyal to England. Many of these people had run away. Now that the war was over, they wanted to return. They could not do so as long as the law against contact with British sympathizers remained.

"I propose that we repeal that law," Patrick told his friend John Tyler.

Mr. Tyler could not understand Patrick's position.

"How can you even think about inviting into your home an enemy who has injured us so severely?"

Patrick did not think of the Tories or the British as enemies any longer.

"We want to see Virginia grow and prosper," he argued. "We need people for this. Many of these people of the Old World want to escape dictators and live in freedom. I cannot imagine any harm they could do, or would want to do."

When the House met, Patrick made a stirring speech. He addressed himself directly to Mr. Tyler, who was then chairman.

"Sir, they are standing on tiptoe upon their native shore and looking to your shores with wistful and longing eyes. Tell them to come, and bid them welcome. I have no fear of any mischief they can do us."

Patrick's voice was a trumpet.

"Afraid of them!" he cried. "Shall we who have laid the proud British Lion at our feet now be afraid of her whelps?"

This was one time Patrick did not sway enough votes to support his resolution. After a time the delegates did come around to his way of thinking. Patrick introduced a similar resolution sometime later, and it passed.

When Patrick went home to Leatherwood, it was with the hope that he could stay there and begin his law practice again. Four children had been added to his already large family.

"It will be a pleasure to have you home where the children can see and get to know their father," said Dolly. "They will begin to think they are orphans."

"The war has left me with very little money," said Patrick. "We are all more likely to find ourselves paupers first."

"That is highly unlikely for a man of your abilities," said Dolly. "Unless, of course, you return to public life," she added.

"My dear, I do not intend to do anything but devote myself to my family," insisted Patrick.

"What if the people should call?" asked Dolly.

"I'll be too far away to hear," said Patrick.

But Patrick was never far away.

12

"United We Stand"

After the war Patrick Henry was elected Governor
of Virginia twice more. He moved his family to an
estate called Salisbury near Richmond, which was
now the Capital.

Dolly knew that her husband could not be
happy unless he was part of the Virginia government.

"At least we shall all be together," she sighed.

"Tell the truth, my dear," said Patrick. "You do
enjoy the parties and the visitors."

Dolly was a charming hostess, and she did like
entertaining.

"I don't mind," she admitted. "I especially like
showing off our lovely children."

By the time Patrick's terms as governor were
completed, there were five children — Dorothea,
Sarah, Martha, Patrick, and Fayette.

During Patrick's last year as governor, he became more and more disturbed about the actions of Congress in Philadelphia.

"There is a rumor that the northern states hope to make a trade agreement with Spain," James Madison told Governor Henry.

"Fine!" said Patrick. "With sound trade agreements our country will grow rich and strong."

Mr. Madison shook his head. "Under ordinary circumstances I would agree with you. But in return, Congress proposes to close the Mississippi to trade for twenty-five to thirty years."

Governor Henry was shocked. "How could Congress consider such a treaty? The North will benefit, but the South will be ruined. The southern states depend upon the Mississippi for transportation. Surely the northern delegates cannot seriously consider such a selfish act."

Southern leaders were angry. When talk began about forming a new and stronger central government, Patrick hesitated. Could they trust the northern states to respect the rights of the South?

"If the Mississippi affair is an example of how the northern states plan to organize our new country, I want no part of it," he said.

Mr. Madison was worried, too. All the states realized that something had to be done about their

government. When Congress tried to raise money to pay war debts, the states voluntarily contributed less than one fourth of what was needed.

The states agreed to meet in Philadelphia to prepare a new plan of government. George Washington and James Madison were elected delegates to the Convention. So was Patrick Henry. No one knew what he planned to do.

"Mr. Henry may not support a new plan of federal government if the Mississippi affair is not cleared up," Mr. Madison wrote to General Washington.

Patrick Henry refused a third term as governor. His family was suddenly enlarged again. Patsy's husband, John Fontaine, died, and she came with her children to stay with Dolly and Patrick.

"I am not only poor, but in debt," Patrick told a friend.

"Return to the law," his friend urged. "Your tongue will soon pay your debts."

Patrick thought that his friend was probably right. He and Dolly moved their large family to Prince Edward County. Here he soon had more cases than he could handle alone. Everyone wanted the services of the famous Patrick Henry.

Two months after his election to the Philadelphia Convention, Patrick sent his answer to the new governor, Edmund Randolph. He refused to go.

James Madison sent the news to General Washington. He also wrote to Thomas Jefferson in Paris.

"The plan for the sacrifice of the Mississippi has been abandoned. But no one knows what the consequences of this selfish attempt by the northern states will be. Mr. Henry's disgust exceeds all measure."

Everyone knew that if Patrick decided to fight a plan of Federal Government in Virginia, that plan would stand little chance of being accepted.

For months the delegates in Philadelphia worked on the Constitution. When it was completed, it had to be approved at a convention in each state. The Virginia Convention met on the second of June, 1788.

From the beginning, it was clear that Patrick Henry would not support the proposed constitution. There were many other leaders also opposed to it, such as John Tyler, George Mason, and Benjamin Harrison.

One of Patrick's biggest concerns was the fact that the new plan of government did not have a bill of rights. He was deeply concerned about freedom of religion, liberty of the press, and trial by jury.

"Mr. Chairman, the necessity of a bill of rights appears to me to be greater in this government than ever it was in any government before."

Patrick was afraid that the states and the people had given up too much power to the central government.

"If you give up these powers without a bill of rights, you will exhibit the most absurd thing to mankind that ever the world saw — a government that has abandoned all its powers — the powers of direct taxation, the sword and the purse. You have disposed them to Congress without a bill of rights."

James Madison, Edmund Randolph, Henry Lee, and Edmund Pendleton answered these arguments. They said that the plan of government strengthened the union. They pointed out that the rights of the individual were implied and need not be stated. They said there was no danger of the Federal Government becoming too strong. The proposed constitution had built-in methods of checking on each of the three branches.

Patrick was not convinced. He spoke at the Convention almost every day. Once he talked for seven hours without stopping. He was tired and not well. He looked older than his fifty-two years.

Repeated attacks of malaria had left him weak. His face was lined, and his stoop was more pronounced.

But on the next to the last day he made such a fiery speech that he appeared to be young again. He told the Convention that it was not just the happiness of Americans that was at stake. He felt the proposed constitution was a serious danger to the rights and liberties of all mankind.

Patrick told the men that all eyes on earth and in heaven were upon them, waiting to see whether they would make the right decision. He warned them of the disaster that they could bring upon the human race.

The next day the vote was taken. The new constitution and a recommendation to add a bill of rights was approved by only ten votes.

Defeated by the slim majority, Patrick promised to support the government and make necessary changes in a constitutional way.

A few years later, Patrick Henry retired from his law practice and from public life. He moved to a large comfortable home called Red Hill. He was offered many honors, but refused them all. He did not want to be Secretary of State under Washington. He refused to become Chief Justice of the

Supreme Court. Some men wanted him to run for President. This, too, he declined.

"I am tired," he told Dolly. "I want to spend my last years enjoying my home and our children." Altogether Patrick and Dolly had nine children.

Patrick enjoyed sitting under the huge trees on his plantation playing his fiddle and talking with his children and his grandchildren.

When Patrick Henry was sixty-two years old, he received a confidential letter from George Washington. Now retired, the former President lived at Mount Vernon.

President Washington was worried about the country. Some of the states declared that they would not obey the federal laws whenever they did not agree with these laws. Virginia was one of these states. President Washington begged Patrick Henry to convince Virginians that they were wrong.

Patrick had led many political fights. He decided that this was one of the most important fights to be won. Although he had opposed the adoption of the Constitution, he worked hard to support it once it was the law of the land. He knew that if the states did not work together, the country would be destroyed.

Once more Patrick Henry ran for the state legislature. On election day in March, 1799, he was to speak at the Charlotte County Courthouse. People from miles around came to hear him.

With a great effort Patrick Henry stood to address them. He was old now, and his voice quavered. But his belief in his cause gave him strength. His words rang out rich and clear.

"United we stand. Divided we fall!"

It was his last speech. He died two months later on June 6, at Red Hill.

"He was the most popular man in all Virginia," Thomas Jefferson said of him.

His head, his hand, and his heart had been devoted to the cause of liberty. No man could have given more.

Some Other Books to Read

CAMPION, NARDI REEDER, *Patrick Henry: Fire-brand of the Revolution*. Boston: Little, Brown and Company, 1961.

CARSON, JULIA M., *Son of Thunder: Patrick Henry*. New York: Longmans, Green & Co., Inc., 1945.

EARLE, ALICE M., *Child Life in Colonial Days*. New York: The Macmillan Company, 1899; re-issued 1948.

GERSON, NOEL B., *Give Me Liberty*. Garden City, N. Y.: Doubleday & Company, Inc., 1966.

HENRY, WILLIAM WIRT, *Patrick Henry*, 3 vols. New York: Charles Scribner's Sons, 1891.

MAYO, BERNARD, *Myths and Men*. Athens, Georgia: University of Georgia Press, 1959.

MEADE, ROBERT DOUTHAT, *Patrick Henry*, 2 vols. Philadelphia: J. B. Lippincott Company, 1957 and 1969.

TYLER, MOSES COIT, *Patrick Henry*. Ithaca, N. Y.: Cornell University Press, 1887; reprinted in paperback by Great Seal Books, 1962.